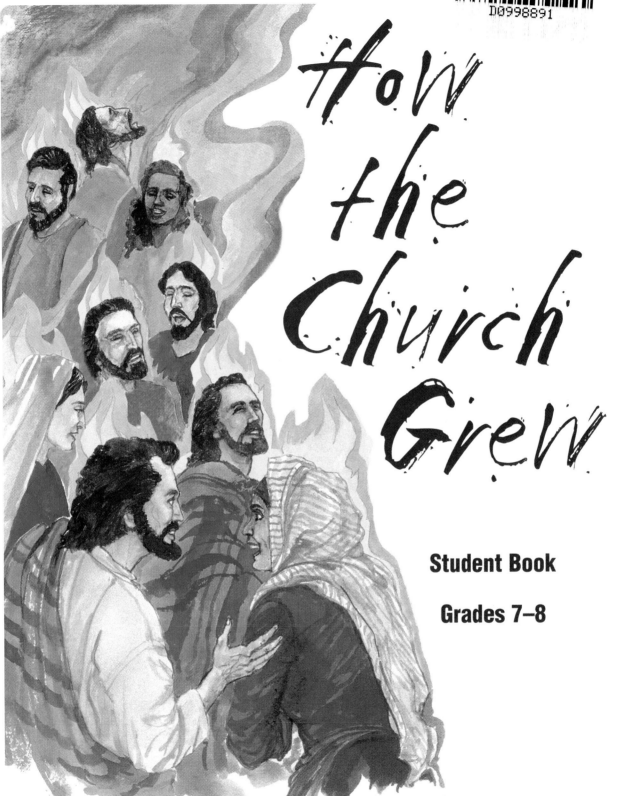

How the Church Grew

Student Book

Grades 7–8

CONCORDIA PUBLISHING HOUSE • SAINT LOUIS

Contents

Editor: Rodney L. Rathmann

Revised from materials written by Norbert Engebrecht, © 1966 CPH.

Scripture quotations are taken from the HOLY BIBLE, NEW INTERNATIONAL VERSION®. NIV®. Copyright © 1973, 1978, 1984 by International Bible Society. Used by permission of Zondervan Publishing House. All rights reserved.

This publication may be available in Braille, in large print, or on cassette tape for the visually impaired. Please allow 8–12 weeks for delivery. Write to the Library for the Blind, 1333 S. Kirkwood Road, St. Louis, MO 63122-7295; call 1-800-433-3954, ext. 1322; or e-mail to blind.library@lcms.org.

Manufactured in the United States of America.

1   2   3   4   5   6   7   8   9   10   12   11   10   09   08   07   06   05   04   03

The fish has been a Christian symbol since the first century. Fish symbols appeared in the catacombs, or underground burial tunnels, in Rome, where early Christians met secretly. At the right is a design from a modern parament, a cloth hanging on the pulpit or lectern, which also uses the fish symbol.

The Greek word for fish (ΙΧΘΥΣ) contains the Greek initials of the words "Jesus Christ, God's Son, Savior." The symbol appears in this book as a reminder that Christians of all centuries are followers of Jesus, the Savior.

IXΘYC

From Jerusalem to Rome

St. Peter by Peter Paul Rubens
(1577–1640)

"But you will receive power when the Holy Spirit comes on you; and you will be My witnesses in Jerusalem, and in all Judea and Samaria, and to the ends of the earth" (Acts 1:8). When Jesus had said this to His disciples on the Mount of Olives, He raised His hands in blessing. Jesus began to go up, and soon a cloud hid Him from their eyes.

The disciples went back to Jerusalem to wait for the coming of the Holy Spirit. Ten days later, on Pentecost, God sent His Holy Spirit on the disciples and all who were with them.

People from many parts of the world had come to Jerusalem for the Pentecost festival. God used a sound like that of a very strong wind to attract thousands to the place where the disciples were. These foreign visitors heard the disciples speaking in their own languages.

Peter was the main speaker. He proclaimed that the crucified and risen Jesus was the promised Savior. The Holy Spirit worked through Peter's message. Before the day was over, 3,000 persons had accepted Jesus as their Savior. When some of these left Jerusalem, they carried the news of Jesus back with them to their homeland.

Persecution

The disciples carried out the Lord's instructions in Jerusalem, continuing to preach and teach about Jesus. The church in Jerusalem grew rapidly.

The leaders of the Jewish religion were unhappy about this. The Jewish council arrested some of the apostles and tried to stop them from talking about the crucified and risen Jesus. But the apostles and other believers kept on testifying of their faith.

View of Jerusalem from the Mount of Olives

Stephen, too, boldly witnessed for his Lord. He worked hard to show that in Jesus the prophecies of the Old Testament had been fulfilled. But many would not listen to him. Instead they rushed Stephen to the council to be tried. They set up false witnesses against him and had him stoned to death.

A heavy persecution of the believers in Jerusalem broke out. Saul of Tarsus became the official agent of the Jewish council. Many Christians were arrested and thrown into prison. Some were even killed because they would not deny Jesus as their Lord and Savior.

Persecution did not stop the growth of the church. God used the persecution to serve a good purpose. The believers were forced to leave Jerusalem to escape their enemies. They fled to Samaria, Galilee, and many places beyond Palestine. Wherever they went they told others the good news of Jesus.

Saul's Conversion

Saul was one of the Christians' main opponents. Saul loved God and His Word as he knew it from the Old Testament. He firmly believed that to say "Jesus is the promised Messiah" was mocking and blaspheming God. He felt he had to do all in his power to stamp out this blasphemy.

"Let me go to Damascus to hunt out and arrest the believers there," Saul told the leaders of the council. They gave him letters authorizing him to carry out his plan.

But on the way to Damascus something startling happened. A dazzling light, brighter than the sun, beamed down on Saul. He heard a voice say, "Saul, Saul, why do you persecute Me?"

"Who are You, Lord?" Saul asked, trembling.

"I am Jesus, whom you are persecuting," the voice answered. "Go to Damascus and you will be told what to do."

Saul's companions led him to Damascus to a house on the street called Straight. Here he spent several days in mental agony. He, Saul, had persecuted God's Son, the risen Savior! Then God sent Ananias to tell him, "You shall be God's missionary to the heathen world."

Paul's Mission Efforts

God had great plans for Saul. Jesus had told His disciples to tell all nations about Him. Saul would spend the rest of his life telling people in distant lands about the Lord Jesus. He would travel thousands of miles to spread the Gospel message. He would face many difficulties and great hardships. And, in the end, Saul would give up his life for his Savior.

Corbis

The Appian Way, a road leading to Rome

GAUL

SPAIN

ITALY

MACEDONIA

BITHYNIA

Rome

Thessalonica • Philippi

GREECE

ASIA

Troas
Smyrna
Ephesus

NORTH AFRICA

Corinth • • Athens

Tarsus
• Lystra
Antioch

CYPRUS

Damascus

MEDITERRANEAN SEA

Jerusalem

Alexandria

EGYPT

Corbis

St. Paul preaching to the Corinthians

For a time Saul served as pastor with Barnabas at the church in Antioch, the capital of Syria. Then the Holy Spirit called them to work among people in other parts of the Mediterranean world.

Saul and Barnabas traveled to the island of Cyprus and to the country now known as

Turkey. At this point the Book of Acts begins using Saul's Greek name, Paul. Paul and Barnabas traveled from one city to another, preaching about Jesus in the synagogues. Usually they met opposition, but the seed of the Gospel was being planted. Many people left their heathen religions and became God's children through faith in Jesus. Christian congregations came into being.

After reporting back to the church at Antioch, Paul was ready to continue his mission activity. This time Silas went with him. At Lystra, Paul and Silas invited young Timothy to go with them. The three visited the churches in Asia Minor established by Paul on his first tour.

Finally they came to Troas (Troy) on the Aegean Sea. In a vision Paul heard a man say, "Come over to Macedonia and help us!" Paul and his companions went to Macedonia and from there to Greece. They worked especially at Philippi, Thessalonica, Athens, and Corinth.

Paul made other missionary journeys, starting new churches wherever he went. He also kept in touch with the churches he had founded, to help and encourage them. To some of these churches Paul wrote letters; these are known as Paul's "epistles."

Paul preached the Gospel in many large cities of the Roman Empire. From these population centers the Gospel spread to the surrounding area. Paul's travels very likely took him as far west as Spain. At least Clement of Rome, who wrote around A.D. 96, says that Paul did reach Spain. This had been Paul's dream, as he wrote in Romans 15:28.

Paul's mission task was never easy. He suffered beatings, imprisonments, and shipwrecks. At Lystra he was stoned and left for dead. Paul's final imprisonment in Rome at the time of Emperor Nero ended in his execution.

Paul used every opportunity to testify about Jesus to others. He considered it a great privilege to carry out the Lord's command to "make disciples of all nations" (Matthew 28:19).

Paul's motto was "For to me, to live is Christ" (Philippians 1:21). In his zeal for Christ, the apostle said, "I have become all things to all men so that by all possible means I might save some" (1 Corinthians 9:22b).

1. Just before Jesus ascended to heaven, He told His disciples to tell about Him to the farthest parts of the world. What did the Lord mean for the disciples to do? How does the church carry out Jesus' instructions today?

2. Suppose you had been one of the disciples at Jesus' time. How would you have felt knowing that the Lord would no longer be with you visibly? Write down a few thoughts that might have occurred to you.

3. Already at its beginning, the Lord provided for the growth of the church. How did He do this at Pentecost? How did the persecution serve God's purpose?

4. Why do you think the early Christians were eager to testify about the Savior? Is this true of Christians today? What opportunities do you have to testify or witness for your Lord?

5. Do you think Paul's mission travels throughout the Mediterranean region took more—or less—courage than the work of missionaries today (for instance, in Papua New Guinea)? Give reasons for your answer.

6. Why did Paul and his partners usually begin their mission activities in a large city?

7. Write a paragraph on the topic "What I Can Learn from the Life of Paul" (or of Stephen).

8. God the Holy Spirit has brought each of us to faith in our Savior, and He guides our lives. The Holy Spirit's work was also important in the early church. Find several instances in the lesson where the Holy Spirit guided and changed people's lives to help the growth of the church.

9. Who were these persons? Why were they important in the growth of the early church?

Peter	Saul of Tarsus
Stephen	Barnabas

10. How does each of these places or terms fit into the story of the early church?

Mount of Olives	Damascus
Pentecost	Antioch
Jerusalem	Epistles
Apostles	"I have become all things"

Prayer

Lord Jesus, thank You for saving me by Your death and resurrection. Use me as a witness to tell others about You. Send Your Holy Spirit to guide me and give me courage. Amen.

Christians Persecuted

The Holy Spirit blessed the spreading of the Gospel beyond the Jews. Christianity spread from the land of Jesus' birth throughout the world, into Europe, Asia, and Africa. Soon there were more Gentile Christians than believers of Jewish extraction. After the death of Paul (about A.D. 67), Christians were persecuted off and on in various parts of the Roman Empire. The Roman government had no official policy on what to do with the growing number of Christians.

When Pliny the Younger became governor of Bithynia in Asia, he wrote a letter to Emperor Trajan. Pliny asked Trajan what he should do with people who were accused of being Christians. Here are his letter and Trajan's answer.

Pliny the Younger,
Governor of Bithynia,
To the Most Noble Emperor Trajan.

Greetings!
When I am in doubt about something, to whom better can I come for advice than to you, my lord?

My problem is with the Christians. I have examined those who were brought to me. I found that they were innocent of any crime except that they have a faith, which our law does not permit. I have asked them three times, "Are you a Christian? If you are, you shall be executed." Anyone who confessed to being a Christian, I sentenced to death.

Many Christians have been brought to me. Some of these have denied that they are Christians. Many more people will be accused before me. What are your instructions, most noble Emperor?

Farewell!

Ruins of the Colosseum in Rome, where Christians were thrown to the lions. At the lower left are underground dungeons where prisoners and animals were kept.

Corbis

8

Art © CPH

Trajan to Pliny the Younger.

Greetings!
 You have done right. No fixed rule can be laid down for each case.
 Remember that Christians are not to be hunted down. Those who accuse someone of being a Christian must give their own name. Any Christian who is brought to you and confesses to be a Christian shall be punished. Anyone who denies being a Christian and burns incense to our gods shall be pardoned.

Farewell!

Trajan wrote this letter to Pliny about A.D. 112. Twelve years later Emperor Hadrian ruled that everyone accused of being a Christian should receive a fair trial. The governors of the provinces in the Roman Empire followed this policy for about a hundred years.

Polycarp

Around A.D. 155 or 156, a great persecution took place in Asia Minor. Some of the Christians at Smyrna were executed because of their faith in Christ. Right after a Christian had been killed by a wild animal in the stadium at Smyrna, the spectators shouted, "Away with these atheists! Find Polycarp!"

Polycarp was the highly respected bishop of the church at Smyrna. He had known the apostle John and perhaps some of the other apostles.

When Polycarp was arrested, the chief of police asked him, "What will it hurt to say, 'Caesar is Lord,' and to burn incense to the gods? Save your life!"

"I will not do it!" Polycarp answered.

When Polycarp arrived at the stadium, the government official urged, "Remember how old you are. Swear by the office of the emperor. Say, 'Away with the atheists!' Curse Christ!"

The Pantheon in Rome, begun in 27 B.C. and rebuilt by Emperor Hadrian in A.D. 120. Originally it was a pagan temple in which Romans worshiped their many gods. Since A.D. 609 it has served as a Christian church.

The Romans used animal sacrifices in their worship. Here Emperor Trajan is shown making sacrifices to the gods before setting off on a military campaign.

Polycarp answered, "Eighty-six years have I served Christ, and He has done me no wrong. How can I deny my King and my Savior?"

The Roman official kept on trying to persuade Polycarp to deny Christ. Finally the official sent his herald to tell the people in the stadium, "Polycarp says he is a Christian."

The people answered, "This is the teacher of Asia. He is the father of the Christians, the destroyer of our gods. He teaches many not to sacrifice to or worship the gods."

At first they demanded that Polycarp be thrown to the lions. Then they shouted, "Burn him alive!" They rushed to gather wood and fuel from nearby shops.

When the executioners wanted to nail Polycarp to the stake, he said, "My God will give me the strength to stand in the flames without being nailed to the stake."

They tied Polycarp to the stake. Then he spoke a beautiful prayer of thanks and praise to God. Soon the flames snuffed out his life.

Why Christians Were Persecuted

The Romans worshiped many gods or idols. They believed their gods had given them a great empire, peace, and prosperity because they were happy over the worship they had received. To keep all these blessings, the Romans felt they had to continue worshiping their gods. It was up to the government to see that people did their duty as loyal citizens.

The Christians would not worship the Roman gods. They would not take part in the many religious festivals and ceremonies, for this would be denying their loyalty to Christ.

The Romans had many statues of their gods. The Christians had no statues. They worshiped an unseen God in a quiet, simple way. Because the Romans could not understand this kind of belief, they accused the Christians of atheism. Atheism, the belief that there is no God, was considered a serious crime against the state.

There was another reason for the persecutions. Many years before, the Roman government had introduced the worship of the "spirit of Rome"—the greatness of Rome and all the blessings this greatness had brought to the Roman Empire. The emperor was the symbol for this "spirit of Rome." To take part in the worship of the emperor was a mark of loyalty.

The Christians would not worship the emperor. To do so would make them guilty of worshiping someone other than God. The Roman government regarded the Christians' behavior as treason.

Christians were accused of other crimes. Because they lived quietly, not participating in festivals and ceremonies, they were looked on as being unsocial. When they celebrated the Lord's Supper, only baptized Christians could attend. The rumor spread that at such meetings they ate the flesh and drank the blood of babies and did many other wicked things.

Corbis

Christian martyrs in Circus Maximus

Art © CPH

A slave makes the sign of the fish to tell a passing nobleman, "I too am a Christian." Because Christians were persecuted, they often had to protect themselves by using secret codes and symbols.

The Church Keeps Growing

At first the persecution of Christians was limited to local communities or areas. Although many believers died for their Lord, the church kept on growing in number and influence.

In A.D. 250 Emperor Decius made a law requiring everyone to sacrifice to the emperor. This resulted in a persecution of Christians throughout the empire. But after several years this persecution came to an end, and the church had rest.

An early church father, Tertullian, said, "The blood of the martyrs is the seed of the church." Do you see why this is true? Early Christian martyrs like Stephen and Polycarp witnessed to their faith in Jesus by giving up their lives. God used their testimony to plant the seed of faith in the hearts of many people. Thus the church continued to spread and grow.

1. How did the Roman governor Pliny deal with Christians, according to the letter he sent to Emperor Trajan? How could Christians escape punishment?

2. It is difficult to be a Christian during times of persecution. Give examples of how young Christians today may find it necessary to suffer or to sacrifice something for Christ.

3. Why would it have been wrong for Polycarp to burn incense to the Roman gods? Do you think Christians today are ready to sacrifice their lives for the Savior?

4. Why did the Romans persecute Christians? Find at least four reasons given in the lesson.

5. We know that "in all things God works for the good of those who love Him" (Romans 8:28). How did God use the persecutions for the benefit of His kingdom? Can you think of an unfortunate event in your life that God turned into something good?

6. What is the meaning of these words?

   martyrs   persecution

   What is the importance of these individuals?

   Trajan   Decius
   Pliny the Younger   Polycarp

7. In the Gospels Jesus tells us what it means to follow Him. Look up the following passages, and indicate what disciples of Jesus should be ready to do:
   a. Matthew 10:37–39
   b. Mark 10:17–22
   c. Luke 9:57–62

8. Look up information in an encyclopedia about the catacombs in Rome, and tell what part they played in the persecutions.

9. We have a record of some of the Christian martyrs of this period of history. Look up and report on one of the following: Ignatius; Blandina; Perpetua; Cyrillus. You may find help in church-history resources such as *The Church through the Ages*, by S. J. Roth and William A. Kramer. (Though it is out of print, your school or church library may have a copy of this.)

Prayer

Dear Jesus, when I am called to suffer for Your sake, give me the comfort of knowing that You always love me and that I am able to share in Your suffering. Amen.

Life in the Early Church

John yawned and stretched. It was still dark outside. His mother had wakened him early, for it was the Lord's Day. Every Sunday the Christians of John's town came together before sunrise to worship. Afterward they hurried home to go to work, for Sunday was a workday.

Soon John and his parents were ready. His mother gave John a basket to carry. In it were bread, a little jug of wine, some olives, cheese, and a piece of woolen cloth. "Our offering for the Lord," his father said.

Soon the three were walking through the dark, empty streets. After a while they came to the door of a large house. Before knocking softly, John's father looked up and down the street. The Christians in their town had not been persecuted for some time, but it was always good to be careful.

"Peace be to you, Demas," said John's parents to the man who opened the door. They walked into the atrium, a large room open to the sky. Others were waiting for worship to begin.

John looked around. Almost everyone was there, including those who were being instructed before their Baptism. Among these were Marcus, one of the town's leading citizens, and Junius, his slave. They would be baptized at Easter.

Worship

At a signal from a deacon, the bishop's assistant, the people walked into a large room. A table with an empty chair behind it stood in front. Several men called elders sat on the side. They helped the bishop with instructing the people and taking care of the congregation.

The men stood on one side and the women on the other. Marcus, Junius, and others who had not been baptized stood at the back of the room.

The bishop, as the early Christians called some of their pastors, stepped behind the table, which served as the altar. "The Lord be with you," he said. "And with your spirit," answered the people.

When the bishop sat down, a reader read from the Old Testament. Then the people sang a psalm. Another reader read from the "memoirs" of the apostles (very likely the Gospels) or from one of the Epistles. Then the bishop explained the Word of God and its meaning for life. After this he spoke a prayer and a blessing.

"Let all who are unbaptized leave," one of the deacons announced. Marcus, Junius, and the others quietly left the room. After their Baptism they, too, would be able to remain for the rest of the service and partake of Communion.

Corbis

This illustration shows the interior of a Roman house. Before there were church buildings, Christians met for worship in such "house churches" as this.

The Communion Service

When the unbaptized had gone, the worshipers exchanged the kiss of peace, men with men, women with women. This meant they were at peace with one another and joyfully looked forward to participating in the Lord's Supper.

At this time John, his parents, and the others came forward to bring offerings of food and clothing. The bread and wine were used for the Communion. Everything else was given to the poor by the deacons.

The bishop spoke a prayer of thanksgiving over the offerings. This prayer went back to the "giving of thanks" by Jesus at the Last Supper. Thus the Lord's Supper became known as "the Eucharist," which means "thanksgiving."

The people stepped forward again to receive the Eucharist. As the bishop gave each a little piece of bread, he said, "The heavenly bread in Jesus Christ." Each replied, "Amen," and then walked to a deacon who held the cup of wine. Upon receiving the wine, each again said, "Amen." After all had received the Lord's Supper, the bishop raised his hand in blessing and said, "Go in peace."

Corbis

A baptismal font discovered in a Christian house-church at Dura, on the Euphrates River. Candidates for Baptism were usually lowered all the way into the water.

Baptism

At the time of the first apostles all who confessed their faith in Jesus as Savior and Lord were baptized. On Pentecost about three thousand people were baptized. These were people who had previously worshiped God at the temple and in their synagogues. They knew the Old Testament.

The apostle Paul usually began his work in a new area by speaking in synagogues. He was concerned to show his hearers, who knew the Old Testament, that Jesus was truly the Son of God and the promised Savior.

As time went on, the life of the early Christians and the witness of their faith attracted a growing number to Christianity. Many of these had been worshiping idols. They had no knowledge of the Old Testament. So they had to be instructed in the Christian faith and its meaning before they could be baptized.

Sometimes the period of instruction lasted as long as three years. The Christians were also concerned that anyone being instructed for Baptism should live as a Christian.

The favorite time for Baptism was at Easter, when the church especially remembered the dying and rising of Christ (see Colossians 2:12–14). The common form of Baptism in the early church was immersion because it symbolized dying and rising again with Christ. Christians also baptized by pouring or sprinkling with water.

The Baptism ceremony took place during the night, before the dawn of Easter. Each person was asked to renounce the devil and all his works. Then the person was led into the water and made a confession of faith in God the Father, Son, and Holy Spirit.

After the Baptism, a drop of olive oil was put on the person's forehead. The bishop laid his hands on the person and said, "In the name of the Father and of the Son and of the Holy Spirit. Peace be with you."

Now the newly baptized was permitted to stay for the full Easter service and to receive Communion, the first of which was given together with milk and honey to symbolize that the person had entered into the Promised Land of God's kingdom. Now, too, the person could bring offerings and join fully in the life of the Christians.

Living the Faith

"See how these Christians love one another!" said a non-Christian. Love of God and people was the mark of the early believers, along with a happy spirit of living for the world to come.

Lucian, a Greek writer, observed about the Christians: "It is incredible to see the ardor with which the people of that religion help one another in their wants. They spare nothing."

The Christians freely shared what they had with others, both Christians and non-Christians. When they came to worship, they brought offerings for the poor and needy. They also contributed money to help slaves buy their freedom.

The followers of Jesus practiced hospitality toward strangers at a time when inns were bad places to stay. They took care of sick people. In

Corbis

Facing persecution, early Christians often met for worship in underground places of burial called catacombs. This illustration shows believers worshiping in such a setting.

times of widespread disease, when non-Christians left sick members of their own family to die, Christians cared for them. Some died of the same disease as a result. Christians also cared for orphans and abandoned children.

At the birth of a child in a non-Christian home, the baby was laid at the father's feet. If the father refused to pick it up, the baby was taken to some lonely place to die. In a Christian home a child was looked on as a gift of God to be loved and cherished.

The early Christians knew that the Lord lived in their midst. They felt very much the joy of living together here on earth as members of God's family. They showed their love for one another as brothers and sisters in Christ.

The great contrast between the life of the Christian and that of the average non-Christian attracted many to Christianity. The number of Christians grew rapidly, especially during the third century. Then came another empirewide persecution of Christians, which the next lesson describes.

1. Why did the early Christians have their worship service on Sunday? Why did they worship before sunrise?

2. In which ways was the worship service of the early church similar to ours? In what ways was it different?

3. In which ways was the Communion service of the early church different from ours? Why was it called the Eucharist?

4. Bishops, elders, and deacons held special offices in the early church. What were the duties of each? Which of these officials compares with pastors today?

5. The Greeks and Romans had slaves to serve them and considered them inferior. Why do you think Christians welcomed slaves into their congregations?

6. All adult converts from paganism had to be instructed for about three years before they could be baptized. Why did the church follow this practice? Describe some of the customs connected with Baptism at this time.

7. Why was Easter the favorite time for Baptisms? Look up Colossians 2:12–14 to find the connection between Christ's resurrection and our Baptism.

8. The early Christians considered it a privilege to join together in worship. Why do you think worship was important for them? Why is it just as important for us?

9. Christians were noted for their love toward one another and for others. Give four examples that show how Christians carried out this love. How did these evidences of Christian love help the growth of the church?

10. Look up Galatians 6:10 and Matthew 5:44. What do these Bible verses tell us about Christian love? List a number of ways in which a Christian can show love today.

11. Write an imaginary diary of a young person who became a Christian at the time described in this lesson. Do not write an account for consecutive days, but space the days to bring out the important happenings. You may have 10 or 15 "entries" in all.

Prayer

Dear God, thank You for loving me and making me one of Your children. Bless me as I worship You in the company of fellow believers. Give me the love I need to help others. Hear my prayer for Jesus' sake. Amen.

Approval by the Government

Early on February 23, A.D. 303, soldiers from the crack Imperial Guard came to the Christian church of Nicomedia, the capital of the eastern part of the Roman Empire. The soldiers forced open the doors of the church. They burned all the Bibles they could find. Then, armed with axes and other weapons, they began to wreck the church. In several hours they had leveled it to the ground. While this was happening, Emperor Diocletian and Galerius, his assistant, stood watching at the imperial palace a short distance away.

Diocletian sent out several orders taking away all legal rights from Christians. He ordered churches to be destroyed, sacred writings to be taken away, and ministers to be jailed and forced to offer sacrifices to the old Roman gods and the emperor. Diocletian and Galerius felt that Christianity posed a threat to the empire and the worship of the old gods of Rome.

A year later Diocletian gave all Christians the choice of denying their faith in Jesus by sacrificing to the gods and the emperor or paying the supreme penalty with their lives.

Roman colossal head of Constantine

For more than 40 years before this there had been comparatively little persecution, and the Christian church had grown steadily. The Christians had been willing to pledge loyalty to the state and the emperor, but they would not offer sacrifices to him and the idols. Now many of them died a martyr's death, although some Christians denied their faith in Jesus during this time of severe testing.

Weary and worn, Diocletian retired in 305. In the troubles that followed, persecution almost stopped in the west but became worse in the eastern part of the empire.

The Emblem of Christ Appearing to Constantine

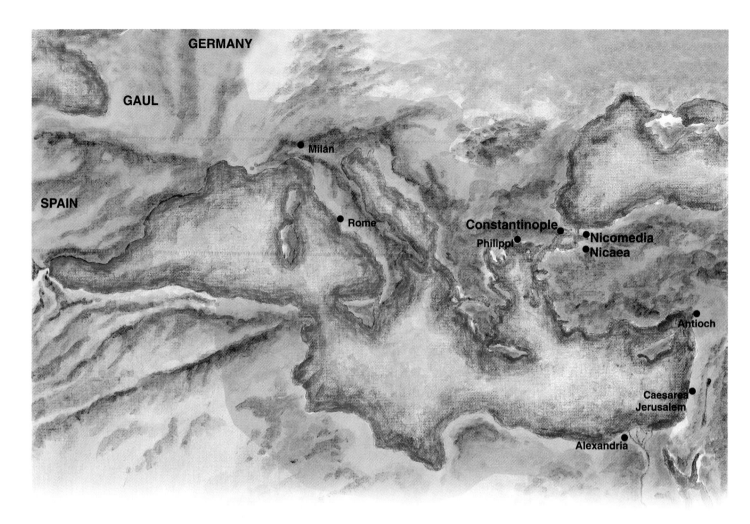

Constantine

Several men wanted to become the new emperor. Among them was Constantine, who was in charge of what is Britain and France today. Constantine's army proclaimed him emperor. But to be emperor, he would have to defeat others who also claimed the throne.

Constantine won several important battles. Then in October 312 he marched his army south to the Tiber River near Rome to fight for the control of Rome and all Italy.

The evening before the battle Constantine is said to have seen in the sky above the setting sun a cross of light surrounded by the words *In hoc signo vinces* ("In this sign you shall conquer"). Constantine took these words as his motto. He had the first two letters in the Greek name of Christ painted on his helmet and on the shields of his soldiers.

Constantine won a great victory over his rival. As a result he became ruler of the western part of the Roman Empire. He felt that the God of the Christians had given him the victory. But it took 10 more years of fighting until Constantine became ruler over the whole Roman Empire.

Constantine and Christianity

Emperor Constantine was a friend of Christianity. In what was called the Edict of Milan he gave Christians the right to worship without interference from the government. This edict, or order, gave Christianity official standing before the law.

Christianity soon became the most favored religion of the empire. Its followers could now worship and serve their Lord in public without being harmed. Sunday became an official day of rest for all. Churches that had been destroyed were rebuilt at government expense. Christian bishops were shown great respect. They did not have to pay taxes and could travel at government expense.

Constantine and his mother, Queen Helena, built a number of beautiful churches. Among these were churches on the site of holy places in Palestine, such as the Church of the Nativity in Bethlehem.

Instead of being tried by fire, the Christian church was now to be tried by the favor of the emperor. The favor he showed the church changed the attitude of many who became Christians. Once it had been hard and dangerous to be a Christian; now it was easy and fashionable. New members flocked to the churches. Often they knew little and cared less about what it meant to be a Christian. They did not have to face persecution. They no longer had to be instructed for several years before receiving Baptism. Many joined the church because this made it easier for them to get a job or because they wanted to please the emperor.

Constantine had hoped that the Christian religion would be the cement to hold his large empire together. He wanted unity and peace in both the empire and the church. But to Constantine's great disappointment, the cement began to crack.

A Quarrel and Its Outcome

A bitter quarrel broke out among the Christians. All Christians agreed that God is one Being. But what was the relationship between God the Father and Jesus? A pastor named Arius said, "Jesus is not fully God, nor is He fully man." Arius believed that Jesus was a sort of half-God. He said, "The Son has a beginning, but God is without beginning." Arius thought God the Father had created Jesus the Son.

Constantine didn't understand what the arguments were all about, but he wanted harmony and agreement. "This quarrel must stop," he said, "or there will no longer be one church but two."

To settle the questions, Constantine called together the leaders of the whole Christian church in 325 at the town of Nicaea, near Constantinople. More than 300 bishops came for the meeting. Constantine came dressed in gorgeous robes glittering with gold and precious stones. He served as chairman.

Arius first presented his views about Jesus. Then a young man named Athanasius, from Alexandria, Egypt, insisted that Jesus was completely God as the Bible states. Athanasius pointed out that if Christ were not truly God, He could never have been our

Interior of the Church of the Nativity in Bethlehem, originally built by Constantine; rebuilt in 527–65.

Corbis

Savior. In the end the church leaders adopted a statement known as "The Creed of Nicaea." It stated that Jesus is "very God of very God, begotten, not made, being of one substance with the Father."

This creed is now called the Nicene Creed. In it we confess that both Jesus and the Holy Spirit are equal with God the Father, yet God is one. Most Christians today regard the Nicene Creed as one of the main statements of what they believe.

Under Constantine, Christianity became a tolerated religion. In 381, emperor Theodosius the Great declared Christianity the official religion of the Roman Empire. But the favors the state showered on the church actually weakened it. Forcing people to become Christians goes against God's Word. Hypocrisy and oppression occurred as a result. The church had lost the first and unwavering faith of the years of persecution. The emperors began to have more and more power over the church. Sometimes they used the church to strengthen their own position. Later centuries would show how well the church stood the test of official favor.

1. What methods did Emperor Diocletian use in his persecution of Christians? Why did he want to wipe out Christianity?

2. Constantine was one of several leaders who wanted to become emperor. What was he supposed to have seen in the sky before an important battle in Italy? What changes did Constantine make in his army as a result of this vision?

3. When he became ruler of the Roman Empire, Constantine issued the Edict of Milan. What did this edict do for the Christians? How do you think Christians felt about the edict?

4. Under Constantine Christianity became the most favored religion of the empire. List some of the favors he gave the church. What did he hope the church would do for his empire?

5. Constantine's new policy also hurt the church in many ways. Why did many people join the church? For what reasons do people belong to the church today? Do you think it's too easy to be a Christian now?

6. What false beliefs did Arius and his followers hold about Jesus ?

7. Who defended the truth that Jesus is truly God? Why is it important that Jesus is truly God?

8. Look up John 1:1–18. ("The Word" refers to Jesus.) On the basis of this passage write an answer to the views of Arius, stressing who Jesus is and what He has done.

9. In order to defend the truth that Jesus is truly God, the church developed the Nicene Creed. You will find this creed in your hymnal. Pick out the parts that particularly emphasize that Jesus is God and equal with the Father. Do the same with the parts that refer to God the Holy Spirit.

10. Constantine did many favors for the church, yet he also harmed the church. Does our government favor certain religions? Is this good or bad? Why?

11. Write a make-believe interview with one of these men: Constantine; Arius; Athanasius. Show how the one you chose responded to the question "What do you think of Christ?"

Prayer

Dear Lord, we thank You for a government that allows us freedom of religion. Give us the strength to live our lives to Your glory and to confess our faith to others. For Jesus' sake we pray. Amen.

Mission Outreach

The story of how the church grew is the story of Christian mission work. Ever since Pentecost Christ's followers have been spreading the news of forgiveness and salvation, sometimes slowly, sometimes more rapidly. People in Spain, for example, believe that the Gospel was brought to them first by Paul and Peter and then by St. James, who was later beheaded by Herod. St. James, or Santiago in Spanish, became the patron saint of the people of Spain. According to legend the apostle Thomas brought the Gospel to India.

Somewhat similar to the days of the apostles, the time of the breakup of the Roman Empire was a time of strong mission outreach. Christianity spread to Ireland, Britain, Germany, and other countries north of the Mediterranean Sea. Several persons in particular played an important part in this mission advance.

Patrick

About the year 405 some pirates came across the sea from Ireland to Britain. The attack was unexpected, and the people of the community could not defend themselves. The pirates burned homes, killed some of the residents, and took others captive. Among the captives was a 16-year-old Christian boy named Patrick, whose parents had been killed.

The raiders took Patrick to Ireland and sold him into slavery. For six years he herded pigs. The young man longed for home. He thought about his Christian relatives and friends. Now he was alone where there were no other Christians.

In his loneliness and misery Patrick prayed to God. He realized more than ever how much he needed God, and he understood better what the Christian faith meant. Patrick wrote: "The Lord opened the understanding of my unbelief that, late as it was, I might remember my faults and turn to the Lord God with all my heart. . . . He pitied my youth and ignorance . . . and He strengthened and comforted me."

One day Patrick escaped and fled to the seacoast. There he found a ship ready to sail. At first the captain refused to take him aboard, but finally he agreed. The ship landed on the west coast of France. After working two months for the traders, Patrick became a free man.

Although no longer a slave to men, Patrick now considered himself a slave to God.

St. Patrick

Art © CPH

He studied for a number of years in a French monastery and then returned home to Britain. His relatives were overjoyed to see him and took him in as their own son. But soon afterward in a dream Patrick heard voices from Ireland calling, "Please come and live among us again." He believed this was his call to bring the Gospel to Ireland.

To make ready for his work, Patrick studied some more in Europe. He was over 40 years old when he set sail for Ireland. He returned to the island where he had once fed pigs—this time to win people for Jesus Christ.

St. Patrick, as he is commonly known, traveled through most of Ireland, taking the Gospel to places where it had never been heard. He also started monasteries, which in turn sent missionaries to other lands. By the time he died in 461, much of Ireland had become Christian.

Columba

From Ireland Christian missionaries went across to Scotland. One of their leaders was Columba, an Irish monk. Columba belonged to a distinguished family. His parents were of royal blood, being related to some of the most powerful rulers in Ireland. But Columba left his home to devote his life to the Savior in a special way.

Like Patrick, Columba founded monasteries for the training of Christian teachers and missionaries. He himself led a group of Irish missionaries to the neighboring land of Scotland. He traveled about with 12 other men, much as Jesus had done with His 12 disciples. Columba's greatest successes were among the people of northern Scotland. The Holy Spirit blessed his work by bringing many of the Scots to faith in Christ.

A view of the Irish countryside as it looks today. St. Patrick worked in Ireland as a slave before returning as a missionary.

Corbis

Gregory and Augustine, Apostle to Britain

One of the most mission-minded men of the times was Gregory, the bishop of Rome. He sent missionaries to the pagan Angles and Saxons who had conquered southern Britain. The story is told that Gregory became interested in these people because he saw some Anglish (or English) boys for sale as slaves. Their blue eyes and blond hair made him ask, "Where do they come from?"

"From the province of Britain," he was told. "They are Angles."

"They look like angels," said Gregory, "and should be won for Christ."

He determined that someone must carry the Gospel to these people. Later he sent a monk named Augustine and 40 other monks to Angle-land. Augustine tried to talk Gregory out of this mission to the barbarians, but Gregory insisted.

It was a long journey from Italy to Britain. There were many hardships along the way, and the possibility of death at the end of their trip worried Augustine and his helpers. When they set foot on England, they found no such danger. Ethelbert, king of Kent, had married a princess who was already a Christian. Soon the king and many of the people were baptized.

The missionaries continued to preach the Gospel

St. Boniface sharing God's Word with the Germans

among the Angles and Saxons. In about one hundred years most of the people in England were Christians.

Boniface

Soon after the English were converted, they sent missionaries to other lands. One of the greatest of these was Boniface, who left his home in England to work among the pagan tribes of Germany.

One German tribe had a great oak tree that was sacred to their god Thor. They believed Thor would strike anyone dead who touched the

tree. Boniface took an ax and cut it down. He was not struck dead. The missionary then split the tree into planks and built a chapel for the Lord.

Many Germans were converted by the work of Boniface. He started schools and monasteries and brought other missionaries to Germany. To the end of his life he continued to witness for the Savior. At the age of 75 he was killed by robbers while performing a Baptism. Because of his devoted labor among the Germans he became known as the "apostle to the Germans."

Within the span of a

few centuries the Christian church had grown from a tiny seed to a mighty tree. At the beginning there were only a handful of Christians. They were ignored, despised, and persecuted. But accompanied by the Spirit and power of God, the disciples multiplied and spread throughout the Roman Empire and beyond. The risen Lord was fulfilling His promise to make His love known to all people.

1. Identify the following. Show what part each played in the church's mission outreach.

Gregory	Patrick
Boniface	Ethelbert
Augustine	Columba

2. Why do you think Patrick thought about God more and depended on Him more after he became a slave in Ireland? Why do many people with luxuries and a comfortable life forget about God?

3. Why do you think Patrick was so willing to return to Ireland? What arguments might some of his relatives have given as to why he should not go back to Ireland?

4. Wherever he went in Ireland, St. Patrick started monasteries. What is a monastery? Why would people at this time want to live in a monastery?

5. Catastrophe came to Patrick early in life. Yet God guided his entire life. Show how the events in Patrick's life were for his own good and for the benefit of others.

6. How did Gregory become interested in sending missionaries to the people of England?

7. How did Boniface show his courage as a missionary for Christ among the Germans?

8. What connection do you see between yourself and the missionaries mentioned in this lesson? What might the work of men like Columba and Boniface have to do with your being a Christian?

9. In which way can God's people best help the growth of the church—by personally witnessing where they are or by sending out missionaries?

10. St. Patrick called himself a "slave to God." Write a paragraph showing how this phrase applied to the life of St. Patrick. Then write another paragraph to show how it applies to your life.

11. Write a short radio play with several scenes from the life of St. Patrick. You may want to tape-record the play for class presentation.

12. Write a missionary prayer.

Prayer

"My gracious Master and my God, Assist me to proclaim, To spread through all the earth abroad The honors of Your name." Amen.

6 Growth of the Papacy

When Constantine was still ruler of the Roman Empire, he changed its capital from Rome to Constantinople in Greece. This move split the empire and began to weaken it. By the year 400 the Roman army, which had long been unsurpassed, was no longer strong. It was unable to keep order throughout the empire or to protect its citizens from warlike invaders.

Attila and the Huns

Among the invaders were the Huns from Central Asia. Led by Attila, they spread terror and destruction throughout Europe. In the year 452 Attila and his warriors swarmed into Italy and threatened the city of Rome. Since there was no longer an emperor in Rome with an army to stop the Huns, the city seemed doomed.

Then Leo, the bishop of Rome, appeared in the camp of the attackers outside the city. He succeeded in persuading Attila to spare the city. Attila took a large ransom, but he did not loot or destroy Rome. The people of Rome hailed Leo as a hero. They gave him the reverence that had once been given to the emperor. Gradually Christians throughout the empire began to look to the bishop of Rome as their leader.

Corbis

The Meeting of Attila the Hun and Pope Leo I by Raphael

Growing Importance of Rome

In the early church all bishops had been equal in rank. A bishop was the pastor, or shepherd, of all the Christians in a city. He would not tell another bishop what to do. At church meetings where false beliefs were discussed no one bishop had more authority than another.

Gradually a change came about. Bishops in the larger cities began to receive a higher rank than bishops of smaller cities. Then the bishops of Jerusalem, Antioch, Alexandria, Constantinople, and Rome were considered of special importance. These cities were among the great cities of the world. Their bishops became known as patriarchs.

For many years there was rivalry among the five patriarchs to see who would be the head of the church. The patriarchs of Constantinople

The Vatican

Corbis

and Rome made the strongest claims for this honor, and Rome finally won out.

There were many reasons for Rome's victory. For centuries it had been the capital city of the empire. People had looked to Rome and the emperor for protection and security. Even after the emperor moved to Constantinople, people still considered Rome the greater city and regarded its bishop as their leader.

The congregation at Rome was probably the largest in the world. It was also very wealthy and had a reputation for helping needy Christians.

Another reason for the Roman church's superiority was the belief that Peter and Paul had been martyred in Rome. The tradition spread that Peter was the first bishop of Rome, though no one knows for sure whether Peter had ever been in Rome.

The church at Rome had many outstanding leaders. Able and courageous bishops stood firm against false teachings. They also sent out missionaries to non-Christian lands. Through these missionaries the new churches developed a loyalty to the mother church at Rome.

The Pope Crowns Charlemagne

About the year 600 Gregory I became bishop of Rome. He claimed that he was the pope, the head of the whole church. From then on the bishops of Rome have taken the title of pope, which means "father."

About 200 years after Gregory a powerful king ruled in Germany, France, and Italy. His name was Charlemagne. Charlemagne asserted himself as leader over both civic and church affairs. He strength-

Charlemagne being crowned as emperor by the pope

ened the empire and worked to reform and advance education. But even Charlemagne considered the bishop of Rome as the most important official in the church. In a letter Charlemagne asked for the pope's blessing and in turn promised to protect him.

In St. Peter's Cathedral on Christmas Day, 800, the pope crowned Charlemagne emperor of the Romans. The pope could now claim that he had power to decide who should become king or emperor. The time would come when the bishop of Rome would not only rule the church but also claim authority over all kings and emperors.

The Muslim Threat

In the meantime a serious danger to the papacy and the whole Christian church was developing. Islam, a religion opposed to Christianity, was sweeping through one country after another and threatening to overrun Europe.

The new religion started with one man, an Arabian camel driver and merchant named Muhammad. On his business trips Muhammad came in touch with Christians, Jews, and pagans. He decided to combine the various beliefs into one religion for all his people. He taught that Abraham, Moses, and Jesus were prophets of God but that he, Muhammad, was the greatest prophet. People had to work out their salvation by performing works such as fasting, giving alms to the poor, and bowing in prayer toward Mecca five times a day.

Muhammad's teachings didn't go over too well with his friends and relatives. Leaving his home city of Mecca, he fled to Medina in 622, the date Muslims (followers of Muhammad) observe as the beginning of their religion. The people of Medina welcomed Muhammad and made him their leader. Within a few years almost all Arabians had become his followers.

The Muslims were aggressive missionaries. They believed in spreading their religion by the sword if necessary. After Muhammad's death they conquered the neighboring countries of Persia, Syria, and Palestine. They marched to the gates of Constantinople but were driven back by burning tar and oil poured down from the walls.

Trying a different approach to Europe, the Muslims swept across Egypt, North Africa, and Spain. They met little resistance as they crossed the mountains and advanced far into France. Just as things were looking hopeless for the Christians of Europe, Charles Martel led

Corbis

Followers of Islam bowing on prayer rugs at one of their five daily prayer times the French army against the invaders. In the battle of Tours in 732 Charles Martel badly defeated the Muslims and turned them back.

The battle of Tours was one of the most important events in the history of the Christian church. If the Muslims had not been stopped, they might have conquered all Europe and wiped out most of Christianity. But God saw fit to preserve His church so that its growth could continue.

An Enemy Conquers and Is Conquered

Meanwhile also during the eighth century, a mighty threat emerged from the North. During this time Scandinavians from the extreme northern regions of Europe developed skill in building sleek, fast ships propelled by oar and sail and able to carry approximately 80 men. Using these ships Norsemen, or Vikings, began to attack and conquer other regions of Europe. Norsemen assimilated well with those they conquered and eventually adopted the religion of those they had defeated in battle, becoming Christians themselves.

1. Tell something about each of the following:

    Attila   Charlemagne
    Huns   Muhammad
    Leo   Charles Martel
    Gregory

2. Why was it possible for Attila and the Huns to spread terror and destruction throughout Europe and even threaten the city of Rome?

3. Why did the people of Rome come to look upon Bishop Leo as a hero?

4. What was the difference between a bishop and a patriarch? Which cities were led by patriarchs?

5. The patriarch of Rome eventually became ruler of the church. List five reasons why he won out over the others. What title did he take? What does this title mean?

6. In the year 800 the bishop of Rome crowned Charlemagne emperor. What additional power could the bishop of Rome now begin to claim?

7. Look up Ephesians 1:22. Who is the real head of the church? Why do we owe Him our first allegiance?

8. What are some dangers to the church if one person or group has a great deal of control over the members?

9. Look up Matthew 20:20–28. What answer did Jesus give a mother when she asked for places of privilege for her sons in His kingdom?

10. Find out as much as you can about Islam. What does it teach about Jesus? What would you say to someone who believes there is no God but Allah and Muhammad is his prophet?

11. Why was the battle of Tours so important for Christianity? Show that God's hand was active at this point in history.

Prayer

Dear Jesus, thank You for coming to serve and to give Your life for all people. Help me be like You in serving others. Amen.

Life in the Church of the Middle Ages (I)

If you were to take a trip to Europe, you would see many large cathedrals. Some of the most magnificent Christian churches are in northern France. They were built during the Middle Ages, when life centered in God and the common people had a Christian world view.

Cathedrals were usually built in towns. The towns were not very large compared with our cities today. Everyone in the town helped build the cathedral. Rich and poor alike gave their offerings for the building. Men, women, and children pulled carts containing large stones. Craftsmen and artists contributed their skill.

We know little about the architects, engineers, and artists. Their fame and honor were unimportant. They designed and erected the cathedral for the glory of God.

As we near the town, we can see the cathedral from miles away. It is very large and high. It dwarfs the shops and homes nearby and overwhelms a person viewing it. This indicates that God and religion were of chief importance for the people of the Middle Ages. God's house had to be the outstanding building in town.

Inside the Cathedral

As we enter the cathedral, we wonder at the quiet grandeur of the style identified as Gothic. The design and great height of the church draw our eyes upward. The builders planned it this way. The upward sweep was to remind the worshipers of heaven and God. The Christians of the Middle Ages hoped for heaven. For them as for us, the earth was but a temporary home.

We also notice that, like churches of the Roman style, the floor plan of the cathedral

Corbis

Nave of a cathedral. Note the upward sweeping design.

forms a cross. The nave (the main section of the church) is the vertical part of the cross; the transepts (the two areas jutting out on the sides) are the horizontal part. It is through the cross that God redeemed people and gave them the hope of heaven. The cathedral was a constant reminder of the importance of Christ's death.

Toward the front of the building is the high altar, carved entirely by hand. All around we see beautiful windows with panes of red, blue, and other brilliant colors. Statues and decorative designs cover the stone walls on the inside as well as the outside.

One famous cathedral had more than 1,800 statues and almost 200 windows. Through them people learned the story of salvation. Most of the people could not read, and the printed Bible was not available to them. They learned about God and His plan of redemption from the scenes they saw on the walls and windows of the cathedral.

Visual Aids

As we follow along, we see scenes from the Old Testament illustrating the creation, the fall of Adam and Eve, the flood, the sacrifice of Isaac, and events in the lives of

Corbis

Stained-glass windows beautify the church while helping to tell the message of God's Word.

Corbis

The cathedral in Chartres, France, dominates the town.

Corbis

Statues of saints and common people adorn the walls.

Courtesy French Goverment Tourist Office

A pulpit with decorative figures above and below

The people of the Middle Ages believed that saints could help them in their problems.

Some visitors to the cathedral are surprised to find scenes from the everyday life of the people. We see illustrations representing the work of bakers, farmers, shoemakers, carpenters, and others. Also pictured are the various subjects taught at the universities. People accepted such decoration in their church building because for them every part of life had spiritual meaning.

The Church as a Ship

The church meant a great deal to the people. Above all it represented a ship that would sail them to heaven. Here they were safe from temptations and evils, which could drown them in eternal death.

Passage on the ship was assured them through the seven sacraments of the church. Christians believed that these sacraments were necessary for salvation. A person's sins could not be forgiven without them. The sacraments were Baptism, usually administered to infants; confirmation, celebrated when one received the sacred chrism (pouring on of oil) and the laying on of hands by the bishop; the Lord's Supper; penance, given when a person confessed his or her sins and did some good work to show sorrow; unction, an anointing given to the dying; ordination, adminis-

Samson and Jonah. There are scenes from the life of Christ—His birth, some of His miracles and parables, His passion and death, His resurrection and ascension. Particularly impressive is the sculptured scene of the Last Judgment. Jesus, accompanied by angels, prepares to take the faithful to heaven with Him.

Also shown in stained-glass windows are legends about the saints. In many cathedrals the life of Mary, the mother of Jesus, was pictured.

tered to those entering the priesthood; and marriage.

To help the people understand the sacraments and other teachings, the church had many symbols and ceremonies. It used incense, fire, ashes, oil, salt, and candles to portray sorrow for sin, prayer, and so forth. In the Middle Ages watching the church service was more important than hearing the words.

Bible stories were often taught by means of plays. Sometimes presented in the cathedral itself, the plays told about the life of Isaac and Rebecca, Jacob and Esau, the conversion of Paul, and events in the life of Jesus. Even if a play did not deal with a particular Bible story, it still presented a spiritual message.

St. Hippolytus, who lived in the third century after Christ, said: "The world is a sea in which the church, like a ship, is beaten by the waves but not submerged." This was also the view of Christians in the Middle Ages, who looked to the church for meaning, refuge, and hope.

1. In the Middle Ages Christians erected large church buildings called cathedrals. How did each person do his or her part? How do we help build churches today?

2. The cathedral in the Middle Ages was much larger than any other building in town. What does this show about religion at that time?

3. Cathedrals were also tall buildings that drew people's gaze upward. Why did the builders emphasize this upward sweep?

4. What useful purpose did the decorative windows, statues, and designs in the church serve?

5. Why were scenes from everyday life pictured on the walls and windows of the church?

6. Why did people in the Middle Ages think of the church as a ship?

7. Which were the sacraments of the medieval church? Why were these sacraments important to the people?

8. How many sacraments do we have? Of what value are they for us?

9. "Watching the church service was more important than hearing the words." Explain this statement. What did the people watch? How did it help them?

10. How do the plays of the Middle Ages compare with religious plays today?

11. What is a religious symbol? Do you have any symbols in your church? Try to find at least five.

12. Find pictures of medieval cathedrals, and bring them to class for the bulletin board.

13. Visit a church in your community that is patterned after a medieval cathedral. Report to the class on your visit.

14. Which buildings are the largest and most expensive in your community? What might this indicate about the values people have? What things do we sometimes consider more important than religion?

15. Write a short composition on "Why Christ Is Most Important in My Life."

Prayer

Dear Lord, I depend on You for all the good things in life. Strengthen my faith so that Jesus will become more important in my life. Amen.

Life in the Church of the Middle Ages (II)

Corbis

A monastery garden

Every day Brother Martin came to the castle to teach Latin to young Robert Baldwin. Robert hoped to be a knight someday, and a knight would need to use Latin. Brother Martin wore a long robe of coarse, brown cloth. He was a familiar sight with his small skullcap. Monks like Brother Martin were well educated and often taught future priests and rulers.

The Life of a Monk

Brother Martin and his fellow monks lived apart from other people in a building called a monastery. They were not married and did not own property. They spent much of their time in prayer and meditation. Some monks became missionaries; others served as teachers. Not everyone received an education during the Middle Ages, but those who did usually had monks as teachers.

Monasteries were frequently used as inns or guest houses for travelers. Those traveling great distances were always welcome to receive food and lodging, whether they paid for these services or not. Medical aid was also available at monasteries.

Monks raised their own food. They often became expert farmers and discovered better ways to plant and grow crops. They also tended cattle, sheep, and other animals.

One of the most important contributions of monks was to preserve the books of the ancient world. Since there were no printing presses, monks copied manuscripts by hand. A copier might spend months on a single book. Among the books preserved was the Bible. Monks wrote on dried animal skins, known as

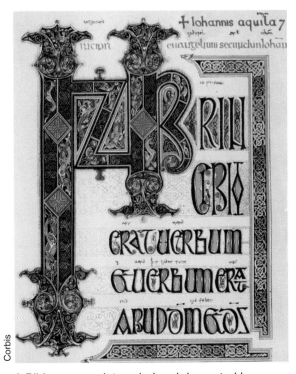

Corbis

A Bible manuscript copied and decorated by a monk in the Middle Ages. This page is the title page from St. John's Gospel.

parchment. They made their own ink and pens. The copier frequently decorated the pages of manuscripts with pictures and designs in bright colors.

The Church and Society

Monks represented the spirit of the church in the Middle Ages. The church's influence on society was stronger than any other influence. People looked to the church to guide them in every part of life. The church pointed out how they could glorify God in their daily work, through their art and music, and in their schools. The church not only showed people the way of salvation, it also helped make a better world.

In many ways the church was the government in the Middle Ages. Kings were not very powerful, and the church took over many of their duties. The pope ruled the city of Rome and the surrounding territory. People looked to their bishop for protection and for help in everyday problems.

One way the church helped society was by establishing schools. Bishops started schools at their cathedrals. Some of these later grew into universities. If a person wanted an education, church schools were usually the only ones available.

The church also took care of the poor, the sick, and orphans. Civil governments paid little attention to the sick and the poor. Hospitals and

A monk giving a crucifix to a knight leaving for the Crusades

Illuminated manuscript with a knight traveling to the Holy Land

orphanages were started and supervised by the church.

Church courts handled many more cases than the government courts did. Religious laws covered just about every situation in life, and the people preferred to be judged in a church court.

A castle built by crusaders during their conquest and defense of the Holy Land

The church also tried to bring Christianity to bear on business affairs. It promoted the idea of just prices. Merchants were not to overcharge when they sold their products. Charging interest on loans was also opposed.

The church tried its best to keep peace and prevent war. In the Middle Ages there was almost constant warfare between knights. In order to cut down fighting, the church promoted the "Truce of God." Knights and nobles agreed not to wage war during certain times. All fighting was to cease during Lent and Advent and from Wednesday evening to Monday morning. The church also forbade attacks on church buildings and other sacred places.

The Crusades

Pope Urban had another idea. Instead of fighting one another, wouldn't it be better for the knights to fight the enemies of Christianity? Let them fight the Muslims (whom they called Turks), who ruled Palestine. This country was important because Christ had lived there. Many Christians went there as pilgrims to visit the holy places. Turks often robbed, tortured, and even killed pilgrims in the Holy Land.

Pope Urban went to Clermont in France and called the nobles together. In stirring words he urged them to drive the Turks out of the Holy Land. "Christian warriors," he said, "don't fight one another. Fight against the unbelievers. All who join the crusade will have their sins forgiven. Those who die will have eternal life."

The knights and nobles were moved by the pope's speech. Here would be a war for Christ under the banner of the cross. From all parts of Europe knights, princes, and common people joined the army of crusaders. In 1099 Jerusalem was taken, but it was easier to take than to hold. The Turks won it back.

Other crusades were organized, but all failed. There was even a crusade made up of thousands of children who left their homes and started a march toward the Holy Land. They never reached Palestine, and many gave their lives for a lost cause.

The crusaders thought they were serving a good purpose. They tried to extend Christ's rule by means of the sword. But they had forgotten this was not the way Jesus wanted His kingdom spread.

1. Describe the kind of life monks lived during the Middle Ages. List five contributions they made. Which of these contributions do you think was the most valuable? Why?

2. In the Middle Ages the church was the strongest influence in a person's life. Why? Is it a strong influence for most people today? Why?

3. Describe how the church spread its influence into politics, education, charities, and the courts. Who is mainly responsible for these areas today? Do you think this is good or bad?

4. How did the church try to prevent war and cut down the fighting?

5. What did Pope Urban suggest to eliminate fighting among Christian knights? What was his purpose in wanting to conquer Palestine? Was this a good purpose? Why?

6. What is wrong with the idea that Jesus' kingdom can be extended by force? How can the world be won for Christ?

7. God doesn't want us to be part-time Christians who go to church on Sunday and forget about our faith the rest of the week. Give examples of how we can apply Christian principles to sports, politics, family life, work, and study.

8. Look up Romans 13:8; 1 Corinthians 10:31; 1 Peter 4:10. What important ideas do these passages suggest regarding a Christian's attitude toward life and toward other people?

9. Write a paragraph on "How I Can Serve Christ in My Daily Life."

Prayer

Dear Father, I can never thank You enough for making me one of Your children. Help me dedicate my life to You that all my actions may glorify You. For Jesus' sake I pray. Amen.

Beginnings of Reform

Jan Hus

For many years the people of western Europe were loyal to the pope at Rome. They had been willing to do and think as they were told by the pope, bishops, and other leaders of the church. They accepted them as God's representatives. But about the year 1200 some people began to ask questions and to wonder whether the pope was always right.

John Wycliffe

One of those questioning the rule of the church leaders was John Wycliffe. Wycliffe, a professor at the University of Oxford in England, exposed the false doctrines that had emerged in the church. He condemned the worldly lives of the priests and monks. He also claimed that some of the teachings of the church did not agree with the Bible. He was the first to translate the Bible into English, a work he finished in 1384. He did this so more people could read the Scriptures for themselves. Wycliffe was declared a heretic, but he had powerful friends and could not be silenced. Wycliffe died in 1384, but his influence inspired those reformers who would come after him.

Jan Hus

Jan Hus was among those inspired by the life and work of Wycliffe. He was a teacher at the University of Prague in Bohemia, part of the modern Czech Republic. Hus was a powerful and popular preacher. In his sermons he condemned the evil and selfish lives of the people and of many priests and monks. He denounced their love of money and luxury, their immorality and pride.

Hus also condemned officials in the church who were more interested in obtaining money from the people than in preaching about Christ. He pointed out that Christ was the real head of the church. He claimed one could be saved without obedience

John Wycliffe

Culver Pictures

Holy Roman Empire

Poland

Bohemia

Hungary

to the pope. Jan Hus became a hero in Bohemia. Many people in that country agreed with his views.

As Hus became more popular, high officials in the church began to fear him. The archbishop of Prague condemned Hus and forbade him to preach. When he continued to speak out against evils in the church, he was excommunicated. Excommunication cut off a person's membership in the church. Hus was also denounced as a heretic, one who opposes the teachings of the church. However, the people of Bohemia rallied behind him.

In 1414 Hus was asked to appear in Constance, Switzerland, at a meeting of church leaders. He was to explain his teachings to them. The emperor had guaranteed his safety both to the meeting and back home again. But when he arrived in Constance, Hus was arrested and imprisoned.

For months he was kept in a dungeon and treated shamefully. He had to wear chains and handcuffs and at night was chained to the wall. During his imprisonment Hus wrote these words to his followers in Bohemia:

I write this letter to you in prison and in chains, expecting tomorrow the sentence of death, full of hope in God, determined not to forsake the truth of God. . . . I know God has been with me during all my troubles. . . . We shall meet again in heaven.

Art © CPH

Corbis

The Burning of Jan Hus

Hus's Trial and Death

In 1415, after six months in prison, Jan Hus was brought to trial. He was asked to take back everything he had taught. This he refused to do, and the council sentenced him to be burned at the stake. He was then dressed in the robes of a priest. The cup for the Communion wine and the plate for the bread were placed in his hands. Then the priestly robes were torn from him and the cup and plate wrenched from his hands.

An archbishop said, "O cursed Judas, who has left the realms of peace, we take from you this cup of salvation."

Hus replied, "I hope by the mercy of God that this day I shall drink in the heavenly kingdom."

The bishops declared, "We give your soul to the devil."

Hus answered, "And I commit myself into the hands of Jesus Christ, who redeemed me."

When he reached the place of execution, Hus prayed loudly, "Lord Jesus Christ, I will bear patiently and humbly this horrible death for the sake of Your Gospel and the preaching of Your Word."

Some men tied Hus to the stake and started the fire. Before he died, he prayed, "O Christ, Son of the living God, have mercy on us."

At the Dawn of Reform

Many people agreed with Hus and Wycliffe that reform and change were needed. Worldliness had taken over the lives of many church leaders. Money and luxury had become more important than spiritual life. Church officials figured out new ways to get money from the people. They charged fees for Baptisms, weddings, and funerals. Important positions in the church were given to the highest bidders. All bishops had to give their first year's salary to the pope. Church leaders spent great amounts of money for beautiful churches, paintings, banquets, and costly robes.

Sometimes church officials were more concerned with gaining political advantage than with ministering to people. Bishops competed with one another for land to rule. For a number of years three men claimed to be the true pope. Christians did not know which pope to follow. Some wondered whether there should even be a pope.

The life of many of the common people also needed reform. Their religious beliefs and hopes were often based on superstition and ignorance. They used religion as magic. The Virgin Mary and other saints became wonder workers to help in time of trouble. Relics of Christ and the saints were supposed to have magical powers. People believed that touching a piece of wood from Christ's cross or making pilgrimages to famous religious sites would help them get to heaven. They also placed faith in

Corbis

The first page of the Gospel of John in Wycliffe's English translation of the Bible

39

the church as such. Loyalty and obedience to the church, they believed, would assure them salvation. The work of Jesus for our redemption was of secondary importance.

Not all church officials and members lived in wickedness and superstition. There were multitudes of devout and sincere Christians. There were many pious priests who served Jesus Christ. Hus and Wycliffe were soon joined by others who were ready to speak out for a renewal of life among Christians.

Corbis

The troubled church in discontented sea

1. Why do you think people in the Middle Ages were loyal to the pope and willing to follow him?

2. Jan Hus was a preacher and teacher in Prague. What criticisms did he make of the church?

3. How did the leaders in the church manage to arrest Jan Hus? Why couldn't they arrest him in Bohemia?

4. What sentence did Jan Hus receive? Was Jan Hus really a heretic? Explain. How do you know he died as a true Christian?

5. How were the views of Jan Hus similar to those of Wycliffe? What debt do we owe Wycliffe?

6. Give several examples to show that worldliness had taken over the lives of many church leaders.

7. The religious views of the common people were often superstitious. Give two examples of superstitious beliefs, and tell why they were harmful.

8. Are people superstitious today? Think of some superstitions you have heard of. Why needn't a Christian worry about a superstition such as Friday the 13th?

9. What is the real purpose of the church? Can you point out how the church of the Middle Ages had neglected its true purpose? Tell what the following Bible passages say about the mission and ministry of believers: Galatians 6:1–2; Hebrews 10:24–25; 2 Timothy 3:16–17; Matthew 28:19–20.

10. What would you think about a person who joins a congregation to help build up his or her business? to be able to play on the church basketball team? because his or her friends belong? For what reasons do you belong to a Christian congregation?

11. We studied about some reforms in the church at the time of Hus and Wycliffe. Can you think of some reforms that might be needed among Christians today?

Prayer

Dear Jesus, I have often made selfish and worldly things too important in my life. Forgive me for the sake of Your suffering and death. Help me appreciate my church as a place in which I can receive strength from You to be unselfish and concerned about others. Amen.

Martin Luther

Luther

Art © CPH

Luther's Inner Struggle

Over 12 years after Columbus discovered America, on July 17, 1505, Martin Luther entered the Augustinian monastery in Erfurt, Germany. Luther had been a student at the University of Erfurt. He had planned to become a lawyer. Now he suddenly changed his plans and set out on a new course. Why did Luther enter the monastery when he was doing so well in his studies at the university?

Martin appeared to be perfectly happy, yet deep down in his heart he was worried about his relationship with God. He had a hard time believing that a holy and just God could accept him in heaven. The medieval church did not picture Jesus as a loving Savior but as a terrible judge who condemned the wicked to eternal hell.

Only by doing many good works, praying to saints, making pilgrimages, and using the sacraments could a person be sure of heaven. The most highly regarded act was to become a monk, forsake the world, and devote one's whole life to prayer, confession, and good works. Luther worried whether he could do enough to save his soul. He felt that God would accept him if he led the life of a monk.

Luther faithfully carried out the duties of a monk. He fasted, sometimes three days in a row. He prayed and meditat-

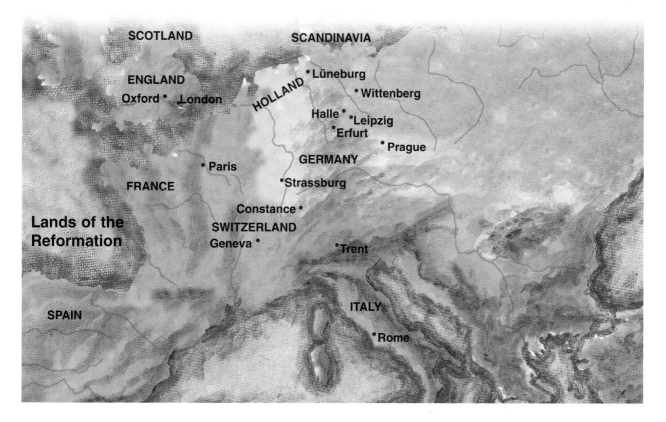

SCOTLAND

SCANDINAVIA

ENGLAND

• Lüneburg

Oxford • • London

HOLLAND

• Wittenberg

Halle • • Leipzig

• Erfurt

• Prague

• Paris

GERMANY

FRANCE

• Strassburg

Constance •

Lands of the Reformation

SWITZERLAND

Geneva •

• Trent

SPAIN

ITALY

• Rome

ed for hours, even during the middle of the night. He slept without blankets and almost froze to death in his cold cell. He went to confess his sins so often that the priest lost patience and told him to stop coming until he had something serious to confess. No matter how many good works he did, Luther was still tormented by the fear that he was a sinner condemned by God.

Luther Finds Peace

Martin went to his superior, John Staupitz, for help in his difficulties. Staupitz suggested that Luther become a teacher at the University of Wittenberg. In 1513 Luther began to lecture on the Book of Psalms. Later he lectured on St. Paul's Epistle to the Romans and his Epistle to the Galatians. In preparation for these lectures Luther discovered the comforting message of the Gospel. It did not happen overnight but took months of study and searching in the Bible.

Gradually Luther began to understand God's love and mercy. God had sent His only Son to take on Himself the sins of all people and to suffer their punishment on the cross. Jesus Christ had earned salvation for mankind, and God offers it as a gift—it costs us nothing. There is nothing a person can or need do to win the love of God. Good works cannot remove sins. Christ has already done this. People can now accept this gift in trust and faith.

Once Luther understood the meaning of Christ's suffering and death on the cross, he had the answer to his doubts and distress.

God had led Luther to discover the true way of salvation. Now he realized that many teachings of the church contradicted the Gospel message in the Bible. But he had no intention of leaving the church or even defying the pope. However, an incident arose that shocked Luther so much he was forced to speak the truth.

Art © CPH

Luther posting his Ninety-five Theses on the door of the Castle Church in Wittenberg, Germany

The Ninety-five Theses

Pope Leo X planned to complete St. Peter's Cathedral in Rome. In order to obtain the money to finish this expensive cathedral, the Pope sent John Tetzel to Germany to sell indulgences. The church taught that after death, believers went to wait in purgatory before going to heaven. Doing good works before death could shorten the time in purgatory. Or, instead of doing good works, people could buy indulgences.

John Tetzel was an able salesman. He preached a thundering sermon and frightened people into buying their way out of purgatory. "When the money clinks in the box," said Tetzel, "a soul flies out of purgatory."

Luther now felt he had to speak out against indulgences. He wrote down his opinions, 95 statements in all. He pointed out especially that forgiveness of sins is a free gift of God. On October 31, 1517, Luther nailed these Ninety-five Theses, as they were called, on the door of the Castle Church in Wittenberg. The door of the church served as a bulletin board. Luther hoped to challenge someone to debate the Ninety-five Theses with him.

The theses had a tremendous and immediate effect. Within a few weeks they were printed and distributed all over Germany. Many people agreed with Martin Luther. They stopped buying indulgences. The pope and other leaders in the church became alarmed at the way the people of Germany rallied behind Luther.

Martin had hoped that Pope Leo would see the evils in indulgences and the way they were used. Instead Leo felt Luther had defied the authority of the pope himself. A number of church leaders tried to get Luther to take back his beliefs. When these attempts failed, the pope excommunicated him. Later he was put on trial before Emperor Charles V. Again he witnessed to the truth of salvation as he found it in the Bible.

Martin Luther (1483–1546) and his friend and co-worker Philip Melanchthon (1497–1560)

Getty Images

NATVS ES ISLEBII DIVINE PROPHETA LVTHERE, IAPETI DE GENTE   PRIOR MAIORVE LVTHER
RELLIGIO FVLGET, TE DVCE PAPA IACET.   NEMO FVIT, TV PAR DOCTE MELANTHON ERAS

43

Luther, Pastor of the New Church

Martin Luther's search for peace of conscience resulted in the Reformation and the beginning of the Lutheran Church. Luther had no intention of starting a new church. He was simply trying to restore the central message of salvation and forgiveness through faith in Christ, the Savior. This was more important to him than any outward organization.

Luther and his friend and co-worker Philip Melanchthon set upon reform efforts to direct all people, including clergy, to God's Word as the means of grace. To help people understand the teachings of God's Word, Luther wrote the Large and Small Catechisms as a summary of Christian doctrine. He also wrote numerous hymns and spiritual songs. The Lutheran church eventually became known as the singing church.

Through the study of God's Word Luther came to recognize marriage as a God-pleasing institution. He encouraged former priests and nuns to marry. In 1525 Luther himself was married to Katharina von Bora, a former nun. God blessed this union with six children. Luther delighted in his children and came to recognize Christian parenting as a high calling.

Luther on trial before Charles V

As Luther grew older he continued to serve God's people as a pastor and teacher, though he became increasingly troubled with illness. He was often called upon to offer guidance and counsel and to help settle disputes. In 1546 while helping to resolve a conflict between two brothers, Luther was called by God to his heavenly home, secure in the knowledge of his eternal reward through the merits of Jesus Christ, his Lord and Savior. Luther's body was laid to rest in the Castle Church at Wittenberg, where he had nailed the Ninety-five Theses 29 years before.

1. Martin Luther was studying to become a lawyer at the University of Erfurt. In 1505 he unexpectedly joined a monastery. Why did Luther change his life's plan?

2. Luther was a faithful and dutiful monk. Why didn't this help him in his difficulties? Debate this sentence: Each of us must undergo the same inner struggle Luther went through.

3. How did Luther discover the solution to his difficulties and worries? What basic Christian truth gave him comfort and peace ?

4. What part did each of the following play in the life of Martin Luther?

   Leo X   John Staupitz   John Tetzel

5. What were indulgences? In your own words write a criticism of indulgences as they were used at the time of Luther.

6. On October 31, 1517, Luther nailed his Ninety-five Theses to the door of the Castle Church in Wittenberg. Why did this become such an important event in the history of the church?

7. Luther realized his sinful condition in the sight of God and was concerned about it. Is sin as serious as Luther made it out to be? Do you ever worry about your sins and God's punishment? Why is it important that we realize our sinful condition?

8. Look up Ephesians 2:8–9. What is meant by "grace" in this Bible verse? What is meant by "works"? Why do we need to be reminded of the truth expressed in this passage?

9. What is purgatory? The Bible doesn't mention such a place. Why isn't purgatory necessary?

10. Write or tell about an experience you have had that strongly affected your faith.

   Special report: Find a list of Luther's Ninety-five Theses and write down the ones you think are most important. Report to the class.

Prayer

Dear Lord, thank You for the gift of Jesus, my Savior. Fill my heart with trust in Him, and fill my life with Your peace. Amen.

John Calvin

The news of Martin Luther's stand for the Gospel quickly spread through most European countries. Many who had been brought up in the teachings of the medieval church supported his views. Especially university students were ready to join Luther in the reform movement.

One of the most important of these was a young French student named John Calvin, who was to become a great reformer. Calvin at first studied for the priesthood. Later he switched to law and the study of ancient Greek and Roman writings.

While a student in Paris, Calvin came in contact with Luther's writings and followed his career with interest. He studied the Bible for himself and realized Luther was right. He became convinced that the Church of Rome did not teach the truth regarding salvation.

Calvin Leaves Paris

John Calvin joined one of the small Protestant groups in Paris. Catholic authorities in that city persecuted Protestant leaders in an effort to wipe out the Reformation in France. Calvin was briefly imprisoned. He decided to leave his home country and go to Strassburg in southern Germany. Here he hoped to follow the quiet life of a scholar and writer.

On his way the 27-year-old Calvin stopped overnight at Geneva, Switzerland. Unexpectedly the local Protestant pastor, William Farel, came to see him.

Farel was a fiery, powerful preacher. He had promoted the cause of the Reformation and

Corbis

John Calvin (1509–64), church reformer and pastor

had established Protestantism in Geneva. But Farel was getting old, and Geneva was a wild, immoral city. He needed help in reforming the people and ministering to them. He believed Calvin was just the man for the job.

A Call from God

John Calvin refused. He wasn't interested in the work at Geneva. He had intended only to stay for a night's lodging and then go on to Strassburg. He considered himself too young, timid, and frail to be pastor of a congregation.

But William Farel insisted and argued with Calvin most of the night. Farel had heard of Calvin before and knew about his exceptional gifts of understanding and thinking, his speaking and writing ability, and his devotion to the truth. He also knew about Calvin's courage and determination in the face of danger and difficulty.

Finally Farel put it on Calvin's conscience to stay in Geneva. He said sternly, "In the name of God I say to you, your studies are a mere excuse. If you refuse to dedicate yourself here with us to this work of God, God will curse you; for you seek yourself rather than Christ."

Calvin was stricken with terror. He gave in and agreed to stay. Afterward he wrote, "It was as if God on high had laid His hand upon me." Such a call he could not refuse.

After a three-year absence, John Calvin returns to Geneva, where he serves for the rest of his life.

Calvinism spread to many countries, including colonial America. The Pilgrims and Puritans who settled in New England were Calvinists. This painting by Jennie Augusta Brownscombe shows a Pilgrim leader offering a prayer at the first Thanksgiving.

Calvin in Geneva

Calvin did not have an easy time as pastor in Geneva. He devoted himself unsparingly to his task and would not compromise the truth. He wanted to make Geneva a model Christian community, "a city of God." He demanded that those who claimed to be God's chosen people obey His laws.

Calvin preached in stern and plain words about the sins of the city. He refused to admit drunkards, gamblers, and thieves to the Lord's Supper until they repented. His strong stand made him popular but also aroused bitter opposition.

Finally both he and Farel were forced to leave the city, Calvin going to Strassburg.

Conditions in Geneva grew worse, and the people began to realize the mistake they had made. After three years they appealed to Calvin to come back. He returned and served in Geneva the rest of his life. His work was very successful. The Gospel took effect in the lives of the people, and Geneva became known for its devotion to Christ.

Like Luther, Calvin stressed the importance of Christian education. He set up schools for the teaching of religion and wrote a catechism, which was used in religious instruction. His most famous publication was *The Institutes of the Christian Religion*. This book presented his beliefs clearly and forcefully. It was read throughout Europe and influenced many people to join Protestant churches.

Spread of Calvinism

Geneva under Calvin became a Reformation stronghold. Protestants persecuted in other lands fled there for refuge. Students came to learn from Calvin. When they returned to their native lands, they established churches based on his teachings. These churches became known as Reformed churches.

Reformed churches were founded in Scotland, England, Holland, France, and parts of Germany. Many of the early settlers in America were followers of Calvin. Puritans from England started the Massachusetts colony; Dutch Reformed immigrants from Holland settled in New York; Episcopalians from England were the major colonists in Virginia.

All through America's history Reformed churches have had considerable influence. Some of the church bodies in the United States that can claim religious descent from Calvin are the Presbyterian, Episcopal, Baptist, Methodist, and United Church of Christ.

1. Why do you think many people supported the views of Martin Luther?

2. Why did John Calvin leave his home country? What were his plans?

3. Instead of going to Germany, Calvin became a pastor in Geneva, Switzerland. How did this change in plans occur?

4. What kind of pastor was John Calvin? How did he show his courage?

5. In which ways did Calvin help spread the Gospel throughout Europe?

6. What name was given to the churches that followed Calvin's teachings? Many church groups in America have a Calvinistic background. Name some of them.

7. Identify: William Farel
   Protestant
   Geneva
   The Institutes of the Christian Religion
   Puritans

8. On the map on page 41 trace Calvin's journeys as they are described in the lesson.

9. Write a letter such as a member of the congregation at Geneva might have written to a friend about John Calvin, the new pastor.

10. Dramatize the scene in which William Farel convinces Calvin to stay in Geneva.

11. Find out about the Presbyterian or some other Reformed church from a member of that church. Report to the class.

12. An outstanding characteristic of John Calvin was his courage and determination. In which situation did he particularly show courage in the face of opposition? Can you think of instances when young Christians today must be ready to stand up for Christian principles?

Prayer

Dear Lord, be with me when I must stand up for You, even if I must stand alone. Help me be stubborn for what is right, that my life may praise and honor You. Amen.

The Catholic Reformation

Before the Protestant Reformation all Christians in western Europe belonged to one church. As a result of the reforms by Luther, Calvin, and others, the followers of these men formed separate churches. Now there were a number of Christian groups, such as Lutherans, Presbyterians, and Reformed. The church led by the pope at Rome became known as the Roman Catholic Church.

Even before the time of Luther, Roman Catholics were shocked at the evils among professed Christians. When many people joined Protestant churches, most Catholics realized that reforms were urgently needed within their church. They also hoped to win back those who had gone over to the Protestants.

Corbis

Ignatius Loyola

Ignatius Loyola

A Spanish nobleman named Ignatius Loyola became the most important of all Catholic reformers. Loyola was born in 1491, eight years after Luther's birth. As a young knight fighting in the Spanish army, he was seriously wounded. A cannonball broke his leg, and he suffered for months.

His leg would not heal properly and twice had to be rebroken and reset. When it finally healed, the leg was shorter than the other. Doctors tried to stretch it out, but this did not work. From then on Ignatius walked with a limp. His career as a soldier was ended.

During his long recovery in the hospital, Loyola read a book on the life of Christ and another on the lives of great heroes of the faith. What he read made a deep impression on him. He now thought about his relationship to God and what he would do with his life.

When he was able to travel again, he went to a monastery, hung up his armor in the chapel, gave away his clothes to a beggar, and dedicated his life to God. Instead of being a sol-

dier for Spain, he would become a soldier for Christ.

After several years of self-denial, meditation, and inner struggle, Ignatius decided that in order to serve God properly he needed an education. He studied theology for seven years at the University of Paris and received a master's degree.

During this time Loyola formed a close friendship with six devoted fellow students. One of them, Francis Xavier, was to become a great missionary. In 1534 the seven men took a vow dedicating their life to the service of the church. This was the beginning of the Society of Jesus.

The Society of Jesus (Jesuits)

Loyola and his friends planned to become missionaries in Palestine but could not obtain passage on ships. In 1540 they went to Rome and put themselves at the service of the pope, who approved their society. Ignatius was elected head of the group.

Jacques Marquette and Louis Jolliet, missionary explorers, traveling with American Indians down the Mississippi River in 1672. Marquette and Jolliet were among the best-known Jesuit missionaries in North America.

Jesuit missionaries served faithfully and traveled far. This missionary brought the Gospel to the south Pacific, where he lies buried.

Music, church litanies, and musical instruments such as this flute were used by Jesuits on missionary expeditions around the world.

Loyola organized the Society of Jesus, or Jesuits, like an army. The "soldiers of God" were to fight under the direction of the pope and give complete obedience to him and to the "general" of their society. Loyola also had written a book called *Spiritual Exercises* for the training and discipline of new members.

The number of Jesuits grew rapidly. Their zeal and self-sacrifice led the way in the reform of the Roman Catholic Church. They established schools and universities and trained great scholars and teachers.

The Jesuits were the pope's "shock troops" against Protestants. Jesuits went to Bohemia, Germany, Hungary, and Poland and won back much of those countries to the Roman Catholic Church. They prevented Protestant gains in Italy, Spain, and France. At times they used torture and other cruel methods to accomplish their aims. Other Catholics disapproved of these methods.

Many heroic missionaries came from the ranks of the Jesuits. Francis Xavier, one of Loyola's early friends, went to India, Japan, and the East Indies. He baptized many thousands in the Roman Catholic faith and was just about to enter China when he died.

Hundreds of Jesuit missionaries accompanied Spanish and French explorers in North and South America. One missionary, Jacques Marquette, helped discover the Mississippi River.

The Council of Trent

The Society of Jesus had made real progress in the program of reform. Roman Catholic leaders wanted to extend the reform program throughout their church. In 1545 Pope Paul III invited all Catholic bishops to the city of Trent to hold a general council. The Council of Trent met on and off for 18 years, making many important decisions.

From then on priests were to be better educated and supervised. No longer would it be

An eighteenth-century print of the Council of Trent

possible for immoral and greedy clergymen to become leaders in the church. An official catechism was approved. The council condemned the teachings of Luther and other Protestant reformers. It particularly rejected the belief that we are saved by faith alone. It also declared that the traditions of the church had as much authority as the Bible. People were forbidden to interpret the Bible for themselves. Only the church could determine what the Bible said.

The Council of Trent approved *The Index of Prohibited Books.* It was morally wrong for Roman Catholics to read the books listed. The pope put the writings of Luther, Calvin, and other Protestant leaders on *The Index.* In this way the spread of Protestantism in Europe was practically brought to a standstill.

1. During the Middle Ages, Christians belonged to one church. How was this changed after the Reformation? What was the church headed by the pope called?

2. At one time Ignatius Loyola looked forward to a career as a soldier. Under what circumstances did he change his mind and dedicate his life to the church?

3. Tell about the beginnings of the Society of Jesus. Show how it was modeled after an army.

4. The Jesuits dedicated themselves to helping the Roman Catholic Church. What did they do in each of the following areas?

   Reform
   Winning back Protestants
   Missions

5. What reforms were made at the Council of Trent? What central teaching of Lutheranism did it condemn?

6. What was *The Index of Prohibited Books?* How did it hurt the spread of Protestantism?

7. Identify each of the following. Why were they important?

   Francis Xavier
   Spiritual Exercises
   Paul III
   Council of Trent
   Society of Jesus

8. Write a make-believe diary of Ignatius Loyola while he was in the hospital recovering from the injury to his leg. Try to reveal some of his thoughts about the past and future.

9. What can a Christian learn from the life of Ignatius Loyola? What criticism of him might you make?

10. Imagine you were a reporter or an observer at the Council of Trent. Write an article interpreting the results of the council.

11. Ask a Roman Catholic friend about that church's beliefs, or read about them in a reference book. Report your findings to the class.

Prayer

Dear Lord Jesus, I know You love me. Thank You for taking all my sins on Yourself. Help me serve You and dedicate my life to You. Amen.

Spiritual Revival

August Francke

Art © CPH

After the first 100 years of the Reformation, many Lutherans in Germany had developed a lukewarm attitude in their faith. Religion had become a routine thing. People were baptized and confirmed, attended church services, and participated in the Lord's Supper but at other times forgot about their religion. They memorized the catechism but did not follow its teachings in everyday life.

A number of pastors in Germany became disturbed about this condition. They tried to help Christians realize the importance of living a pious life. As a result they were called Pietists. Among them was August Francke.

August Francke

Brought up in a religious home, Francke decided while still a boy to become a pastor. As a young man he was dissatisfied with his spiritual life. In 1687 he went to Lüneburg, where he studied the Bible with outstanding, devout teachers. During his brief stay at Lüneburg Francke experienced what he called his "conversion." He was now ready to serve Christ with his whole heart.

Francke returned to the University of Leipzig, where he had formerly taught. He formed a Bible club for devotional study of the Scriptures.

His biblical lectures and sermons emphasized people's need for God's grace. He also urged people to live their Christianity.

Francke attracted a large following, but opposition developed at the university. Authorities prohibited the Bible club meetings and did not allow him to teach religion.

INDIA

Lutheran missionaries Pluetschau and Ziegenbalg brought the Good News of Jesus to the people of India in the eighteenth century. This illustration from the time shows Indian nobility celebrating a pagan religious festival.

Christian missionaries continue to experience opposition to the Gospel. Here a cow—sacred to the Hindu religion—ventures close to a Christian shrine.

Eventually he was forced to leave Leipzig. After spending a year in Erfurt, Francke secured a position as pastor in a town near Halle and became a professor at the University of Halle. Here he found sympathy for his ideas, and the university became a center of Pietism.

Francke's Achievements

Francke was a hard worker and a good organizer. He faithfully served his congregation and tried to practice what he preached. In 1695 he began a school for poor children.

Later he started an orphanage and a high school. These schools became known throughout Germany. Following Francke's religious principles, they emphasized

55

devotional study of the Bible and a life of service to God.

Pastor Francke had little money of his own to support these schools. In answer to his prayers, people from all over Germany sent contributions to support them. The schools grew rapidly. At the time of Francke's death 2,200 children were receiving an education under his direction. In 1710 he started a Bible institute for the publication of inexpensive Bibles. Most of his schools, as well as the Bible institute, have continued to the present.

Francke and the other Pietists were also very interested in mission work. They aroused a missionary zeal in the hearts of their followers. When the king of Denmark needed missionaries to send to India, he enlisted two of Francke's students in Halle. Bartholomew Ziegenbalg and Heinrich Pluetschau became the first Lutheran missionaries to India.

From 1700 to 1800 over 60 men from Halle served as foreign missionaries. In 1742 Henry Muhlenberg came from this German community to Pennsylvania. He was the first great organizer of Lutherans in America.

John and Charles Wesley

In England two brothers, John and Charles Wesley, carried out a similar revival of religious life. They worked against widespread unbelief and low moral conditions in that country. Even the clergy were more interested in the pleasures of hunting, drinking, and eating than in their spiritual duties.

Corbis

Sketch of a Methodist camp meeting at Sing Sing, New York. Outdoor revival meetings were common among followers of the Wesleys.

While attending Oxford University in 1729, the Wesleys helped organize a club for the purpose of growing in their Christian faith and life. They met daily for prayer, studied the Bible, visited prisoners in jail, and fasted.

Other students ridiculed them and called them the "Holy Club." Someone suggested the name "Methodists" because they followed a strict method in their devotions. The name stuck and was later adopted by the church body that grew out of the movement, known today as the Methodist Church.

In 1735 the Wesley brothers sailed to America in answer to a plea for missionaries in Georgia. They worked hard but met with little success and returned to England. John Wesley was disappointed with himself. He felt he had only a fair-weather religion. Something was lacking, for he was afraid in the face of danger and death.

Then in London one evening John found his answer. He went to a meeting of a Christian study group. Martin Luther's introduction to the Book of Romans was being read. Wesley himself relates, "While I was listening to Luther's description of the change which God works in the heart through faith in Christ, I felt I did trust in Christ, Christ alone, for salvation; and an assurance was given me that He had taken away my sins."

John Wesley had found peace in his heart. His brother Charles had had a similar experience only a few days earlier.

Corbis

John Wesley

Beginning of Methodism

The Wesley brothers decided they would dedicate their lives to preaching the Gospel. Since most churches were closed to them, they preached outdoors. Their services were somewhat like revival meetings today. Thousands of people flocked to hear them. Sometimes they were jeered at and howled down. Mobs threw stones at them and threatened their lives, but the Wesleys kept on preaching.

John Wesley himself preached 40,000 sermons and traveled about 225,000 miles on horseback through England, Scotland, Wales, and Ireland. He organized his converts into societies to help and encourage one another and to carry the Gospel message to others.

Charles Wesley wrote over 6,000 hymns, many of which are sung today by English-speaking Christians. Among the most famous are "Jesus, Lover of My Soul"; "Christ the Lord Is Risen Today"; and "Hark! the Herald Angels Sing."

The Methodism of John and Charles Wesley had a wide influence throughout the world. Methodism spread rapidly in the United States and became one of the country's largest religious movements. It founded and promoted the Sunday school and helped in prison reform. It fought slavery and sponsored various charities.

Both Pietists and Methodists brought about a revival in Christian life. They encouraged Bible reading and personal witnessing. They emphasized the work of the Holy Spirit in changing people. They stressed consecration of life to God and reawakened interest in foreign missions.

But the Pietists and Methodists met with criticism that their religion was based too much on feeling and emotion and that they neglected certain important teachings of the Bible. At times they seemed to separate themselves from other Christians, thinking they were "better." Sometimes they overemphasized good works and rules for Christian living. But on the whole the Pietist and Methodist Movements performed a service of great value for Christianity.

1. Describe the spiritual conditions in Germany that disturbed some pastors. What did these pastors do, and what were they called?

2. While August Francke was at Lüneburg, he underwent a spiritual change. What do you think this change was like? Can you think of any person who underwent a similar change in Bible history?

3. What kind of activities did Francke engage in at the universities of Leipzig and Halle? How did the Pietists show their missionary zeal?

4. What religious conditions in England disturbed John and Charles Wesley? How did the Wesley brothers try to promote a deeper spiritual life?

5. How did John Wesley have an experience similar to Francke's "conversion" at Lüneburg?

6. What kind of church services did the Wesley brothers conduct? What difficulties did they face? What name was given to the church group that grew out of their activity?

7. Find at least four hymns by Charles Wesley in your hymnal.

8. What were some of the good things the Pietists and Methodists stressed? What were some of their weaknesses?

9. Why will a true believer not be content with learning about Bible teachings and going to church on Sunday? How will a believer's life reflect his or her faith?

10. Look up 2 Corinthians 5:14–17 and Ephesians 2:10. Point out key words in these Bible passages that show the importance of living a Christian life and the power that enables us to do it.

11. Imagine you are a student at Halle while August Francke is a professor there. Write a letter to a friend telling about Francke's influence.

12. Imagine you are a reporter attending a "revival meeting." Write a first-person news article describing your experience.

Prayer

Holy Spirit, give me a stronger faith and the courage to live for Jesus in all I do. I ask it for the sake of Him who died and rose again for me. Amen.

14 Henry Muhlenberg

After Columbus discovered America, Europeans left their home countries to settle in the new world. Before the Mayflower sailed from Europe, a number of Lutherans had already arrived in America. From then on they came over in ever-increasing numbers.

Some Lutherans emigrated to escape religious persecutions or the ravages of war. Others came to the new world for business reasons. Lutherans from Sweden settled in the colony of Delaware, Dutch Lutherans lived in New York, and persecuted Austrian Lutherans came to Georgia. The Germans, who settled in Pennsylvania, were the largest group.

Art © CPH

Muhlenberg

A Plea for Help

The lack of pastors and teachers was a serious problem facing the scattered Lutherans in America. They depended on the churches in Europe to supply them, and often the supply did not keep up with the need. Sometimes fake pastors tried to take advantage of the situation. In 1733 a number of congregations in Pennsylvania sent a delegation of three men to England and Germany to plead for help.

No one was sent to Pennsylvania until 1741, when Henry Muhlenberg accepted the call. Muhlenberg had graduated from college in Germany with the thought of becoming a missionary to India. These plans did not work out, and he became a pastor and teacher in Saxony.

Two years later he visited a friend in Halle, Pastor G. A. Francke (son of August Francke). This man told Muhlenberg about conditions in Pennsylvania and asked him if he would be willing to go to America. Francke knew that Muhlenberg possessed the qualities for such a position. He was a sincere Christian, tactful, physically strong, and mentally gifted. Muhlenberg was interested and accepted. "If it is the Lord's will, I will go," he said.

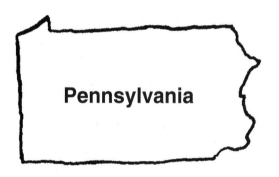

Pennsylvania

Muhlenberg in Pennsylvania

After saying farewell to his family, Muhlenberg sailed for America. The voyage lasted 110 days. He recorded the arrival in his notebook: "In the morning about eight o'clock we arrived in Philadelphia and at first did not know which way to turn." At first no one knew about 31-year-old Pastor Muhlenberg, but he soon won the loyalty of the farmers in the three congregations he served.

The Lord blessed his work. His sincerity and personality won him the respect of the people. They crowded to hear his sermons, which were usually 45 minutes long. After the sermon he would ask questions of the whole congregation on its main points. The Indians named him "Gachswungaroracks," which means, "The preacher whose words should go through hard hearts of men like a saw through a gnarled tree."

The early Lutherans in Pennsylvania did not have church buildings. One congregation held services in an old butcher shop, another in a log house, and the third in a barn. Sometimes Pastor Muhlenberg preached outside under the open sky. One of his earliest undertakings was to erect houses of worship. Some were built of stone and took years to complete.

Muhlenberg organized his congregations in an orderly manner. His constitution for a Lutheran congregation became a model for other churches. He was also interested in the religious education of the young and started Christian schools. Pastor Muhlenberg himself often taught the catechism in the classroom.

Muhlenberg worked at first without a regular salary, but the farmers were generous with provisions. He wrote, "One man brings me a sausage, another a piece of meat, a third a chicken, a fourth a loaf of bread, a fifth some

60

pigeons, a sixth rabbits, a seventh eggs." For rent, clothing, and new horses he ran into debt, but he did not complain. "Our trust is in the living God," he said.

Pennsylvania was still wide-open country, and Muhlenberg had to travel great distances to reach his members. His two country churches were 30 miles from the congregation in Philadelphia and 10 miles from each other. Some families were 30 miles from their nearest Lutheran neighbors.

Preaching, teaching, visiting the sick, performing Baptisms, and conducting funerals required considerable traveling. Muhlenberg hardly had a day at home, spending most of his time on horseback. His travels took him through pathless forests, over mountains, across swollen streams, through ice and snow.

"The Church Must Be Planted"

Muhlenberg took as his motto "The church must be planted." He believed it was his duty to help the scattered Lutherans throughout Pennsylvania and other colonies. He opened new mission stations and assisted other ministers and congregations. He visited Lutherans in New York City, New Jersey, Maryland, and Georgia. Wherever he went he inspired new spiritual life.

Muhlenberg realized that American Lutherans could not always depend on European Lutherans for their pastors and teachers but must begin to train their own. Muhlenberg himself took gifted young men into his home and trained them for the ministry. He even had plans to build a seminary.

It was largely through the efforts of Henry

Corbis

This illustration shows Philadelphia as it might have appeared in Muhlenberg's day. Muhlenberg traveled far from his congregation in Philadelphia to serve Lutheran families and establish congregations in outlying rural areas.

Muhlenberg that the first Lutheran synod was organized. He realized the importance of union and worked untiringly to bring Lutheran congregations together. In 1748 six pastors and 24 laypeople held a meeting in Philadelphia. They formed a synod made up of 10 congregations and adopted a liturgy for their church services.

The synod had a small beginning, but it grew rapidly. It later became part of a large church body known today as the Evangelical Lutheran Church in America. When Henry Muhlenberg died in 1787, there were 25 pastors and 5,000 Lutherans in the mid-Atlantic states. With the Holy Spirit's blessing, Muhlenberg's dream of helping plant the church in America had come true.

1. For what reasons did people from Europe come to live in America? In which colonies did Lutherans settle?

2. Why did Lutheran churches in America have a shortage of pastors and teachers?

3. Henry Muhlenberg hoped to become a missionary to India. Tell how he decided to come to America. To which colony did he come?

4. In what kinds of buildings did Muhlenberg's congregations worship? What were his sermons like? Why do you think Pastor Muhlenberg was interested in schools?

5. Muhlenberg lived in the days before America obtained its independence. Why was it necessary for a pastor to travel great distances?

6. How did Muhlenberg serve other churches besides his own?

7. Muhlenberg helped organize the first Lutheran synod in America. What is a synod? Of what value was a synod in colonial times? Of what value is a synod today?

8. What kind of person was Henry Muhlenberg? Indicate the qualities you admire in him.

9. Write an imaginary diary of five days (not necessarily consecutive) in the life of Muhlenberg. You may describe from his viewpoint any of the events and activities in his career.

10. Write a dramatic skit portraying Muhlenberg's visit to some lonely Lutheran families in one of his country parishes. For weeks they have had no contact with their pastor or fellow members. What things might they ask about? How might their pastor serve their spiritual needs? The skit may be presented in class.

11. Three of Muhlenberg's sons (Frederick, Henry, and Peter) became famous Americans. Find out about them in an encyclopedia, and report their achievements.

12. What is a pastor's main mission? See John 21:15–17. What is the ideal relationship between congregation members and their pastor? See 1 Thessalonians 5:12–13.

Prayer

Dear Lord, thank You for giving us pastors and teachers who tell us about our Savior and His love for us. Bless their work and keep them faithful and strong through the power of Your Spirit. Amen.

Founders of the Missouri Synod

Almost exactly a century after Henry Muhlenberg began his work among Lutherans in the eastern colonies, the founders of another large Lutheran body settled in the central United States. The Lutheran Church—Missouri Synod traces its origin to the arrival of Saxon immigrants to Missouri in 1839.

The Saxon Lutherans

It was for religious freedom that a group of Lutherans left Saxony, a province in Germany. For years these Saxons had not been allowed to worship God as they believed right. The government controlled the church and decided where pastors should serve.

Most officials in the church did not accept the Bible as God's Word or believe that Jesus redeemed us with His death on the cross. The official hymnbook, catechism, and liturgy reflected this viewpoint. Pastors who accepted the Bible had difficulty obtaining an appointment to a congregation. They were even fined or imprisoned.

Friends of the persecuted pastors were so disturbed that they decided to move to America. Here their faith would not be in danger, for the government would permit them to worship God as their conscience directed.

In November 1838 five ships carrying 665 passengers left Germany for St. Louis, Missouri. The leader was Martin Stephan, pastor of St. John's Church in Dresden. Among the persons making the trip were pastors, teachers, lawyers, doctors, businessmen, artists, and farmers.

Arrival in Missouri

After two months the immigrants reached New Orleans. One of the ships was lost at sea and apparently went down with all on board in a heavy storm. The passengers of the other four

The Saxons landing in St. Louis, Missouri

Courtesy Concordia Historical Institute

ships traveled from New Orleans to St. Louis on river steamers.

Pastor Stephan purchased several thousand acres of land in Perry County, 100 miles south of St. Louis. While most of the Saxons settled in Perry County, 120 persons stayed in St. Louis and formed Trinity Lutheran Church.

The Perry County Saxons had a hard time making a living off the poor farmland. They lived in tents and shacks, which became overcrowded and did not protect them adequately against the weather. Food and water supplies were short, and some people died of malaria.

But the most serious problems facing the colony were spiritual ones. Pastor Stephan had persuaded the group to give him the title of bishop and to entrust him with complete authority. But in May 1839 Stephan was accused of immoral conduct and deported from the colony.

The immigrants now had doubts about their entire course of action. Many felt they had acted unwisely in coming to America. They were not sure they were true Christians who had a

Pastor Martin Stephan

A replica of the first Missouri Synod seminary in Perry County, Missouri. Seven students attended the log-cabin school at its beginning.

right to call pastors to administer the Sacraments. Such uncertainty troubled them for almost two years.

C. F. W. Walther

A young pastor, Carl F. W. Walther, guided the Lutherans out of their spiritual difficulties. He showed from the Bible that the true church is found wherever God's Word is taught and believed. He pointed out that any Christian congregation has the right to call pastors.

From this time on Walther was the leader of the Lutherans in Missouri. He became pastor of Trinity Church in St. Louis and gained a wide reputation as a preacher.

In 1844 he began publishing a paper called *Der Lutheraner*. The paper was a powerful instrument for spreading the teachings of the Bible as held by Walther and his followers. *Der Lutheraner* attracted wide attention throughout the Midwest and helped bring scattered Lutherans together.

F. Wyneken

It was through *Der Lutheraner* that Walther and his group came in contact with Pastor Frederick Wyneken. Wyneken had come from Germany six months before the Saxon immigrants. He served as a pioneer missionary in northern Indiana, southern Michigan, and Ohio. Traveling hundreds of miles on horseback, he preached, taught, baptized children, and visited the sick.

Wyneken found Lutherans who had been without the care of a pastor so long that they were in danger of losing their faith. He was ready to endure any hardship to keep these people with their Savior. When Wyneken first read a copy of Walther's *Lutheraner*, he was happy to find other Lutherans who believed and taught as he did.

Pastor Carl F. W. Walther

J. K. Wilhelm Löhe

Wyneken soon realized that one man could not minister to the people in such a large area as he served. In 1841 he returned to Germany to appeal for more missionaries. He found an interested and concerned friend in Pastor Wilhelm Löhe.

Löhe did not come to America himself but sent missionaries to this country. He organized several groups of colonists, who settled in Frankenmuth, Michigan. Löhe also started a seminary at Fort Wayne, Indiana, for the training of pastors in America.

Pastor Löhe was particularly interested in mission work among American Indians. He urged the settlers in Michigan to share the Gospel with the Indians and to set them an example of Christian living. Schools were started for Indian children, and religious books were translated into native dialects.

Missouri Synod Founded

Löhe encouraged Wyneken and the pastors he sent to America to establish closer relations with the Saxons in Missouri. Most of them knew the beliefs of Walther from *Der Lutheraner.* Many of them had corresponded with him and were in agreement with him.

In May 1846 representatives of the Löhe group and the Saxons met in St. Louis to consider organizing a synod. They drew up and discussed a constitution. Another meeting in Fort Wayne completed preliminary work on the constitution.

On Sunday, April 25, 1847, a convention to organize the synod began in Chicago. The most important reasons for joining together were to preserve unity in faith and doctrine and to promote missions and Christian education. The new organization was called the German Evangelical Lutheran Synod of Missouri,

Ohio, and Other States. Pastor Walther was elected the first president.

Only 12 congregations were charter members of the Missouri Synod. But in time it was to become one of the largest and most vigorous groups of Lutherans in the United States and Canada. Hallmarks of the Missouri Synod include an understanding of God's Word that emphasizes the proper distinction between Law and Gospel and an emphasis on Christian education and outreach.

1. Describe the religious conditions in Saxony that led a large group of Lutherans to emigrate to America.

2. How many ships and passengers set out for America? In which part of the country did they settle? Who was their leader?

3. The Lutheran settlers from Saxony faced all the hardships of pioneer life. Describe some of these hardships.

4. What spiritual problems and doubts did the people have?

5. Pastor Carl Walther helped them resolve their problems and doubts. How did he do this?

6. What was *Der Lutheraner?* Why was it important?

7. One of those who came in contact with *Der Lutheraner* was Frederick Wyneken. What kind of work was Pastor Wyneken doing?

8. What were some of the results of the efforts of Wilhelm Löhe ?

9. For what reasons did Wyneken, Walther, and others want to start a synod? How many congregations joined the new synod when it was organized? Who was its first president?

10. One of the blessings God has given us is freedom of religion. Saxon Lutherans came to the United States because its government would not interfere with their beliefs. Write a paragraph explaining what this freedom means to you.

11. Write a dramatic skit reenacting the meeting of Lutherans in Saxony at which they decided to emigrate to America.

12. Write an editorial that could have appeared in *Der Lutheraner* on the founding of the Missouri Synod.

13. Find out how many congregations belong to The Lutheran Church—Missouri Synod today. Who is president now? (See *The Lutheran Annual* or www.lcms.org.)

14. Look up John 8:31–32. In which way did the Saxon Lutherans carry out these words of Jesus? What can we do to follow them?

Prayer

Dear Jesus, thank You for teaching me about Your goodness and love. Give me the strength to be loyal to You and to continue in Your Word. Amen.

'16 Problems and Challenges Today

Corbis

Mary and Shantae were going from house to house in their neighborhood. They asked people about their church membership and talked to them about Christ the Savior. Their pastor had encouraged them in confirmation class to take part in this religious survey, together with the church's regular evangelism callers. As the girls testified about their Savior, sometimes they were happy at people's response. At other times they were disappointed.

The next week Mary and Shantae discussed the visits with Pastor Miller. They told about their disappointing experiences. Some people were indifferent and even discourteous. Others said they hadn't joined a Christian church because so many church members did not live their faith. Still others remained uncommitted because there were too many denominations.

Pastor Miller explained to his young friends that anyone who witnesses for Christ has to expect such responses. He also said that their experiences indicated some of the problems and challenges facing the Christian church in our day.

Indifference and Worldliness

One of the greatest problems is indifference toward the church and its message of forgiveness and salvation. Money, entertainment, and the easy comforts of life have become so important to many people that religion seems old-fashioned to them. They do not care about God and think they can do without Him.

Also, Christians are often more interested in self-satisfaction than in seeking God's kingdom. A Lutheran pastor from Hong Kong on a visit to America said, "As a Chinese refugee in Hong Kong, I learned Christianity from missionaries who were always talking and working for Christ. I thought that was the way all Americans were. But soon after I landed here in your country, I found out differently. Many Americans—Christians too—seemed concerned only with

Corbis

Corbis

questions. Acts 4:12 records, "Salvation is found in no one else, for there is no other name under heaven given to men by which we must be saved." Those who trust in Jesus as their Savior may evidence the results of the fall into sin in their lives, just as everyone else does, but there is one important difference—they know that Jesus has forgiven them through His innocent life and substitutionary death. As the Holy Spirit changes lives through the Word and Sacraments, God's people do "shine like stars" (Philippians 2:15) in the darkness of the unbelieving world around them. Throughout history when the Gospel takes hold, lives change and people begin to treat all others as worthy of dignity and respect. Slavery is eliminated, the status of

money, sex, and sports."

Jesus' followers today have a challenge to be different from the world around them, as the early Christians were; to center their lives in God, as the medieval Christians did; to be fully committed to Christ, as were the missionaries and heroes of the church through the centuries.

The Only Way

Mary and Shantae heard people say that most believe what they are brought up to believe and that basically, all religions are the same. Another comment was that so many church members fail to live their faith. For instance, Christians who profess that Jesus has redeemed all people don't seem any different than those who follow other belief systems. Even many who call

themselves atheists perform kind, charitable acts and practice good citizenship. Yet God's Word is clear—Jesus is the only answer to life's perplexing

Corbis

Corbis

women raised, and all human life is respected.

Non-Christians said of the early believers, "See how they love one another." The challenge to believers today is to show love and concern so that the Gospel may be proclaimed and all people come to know Jesus as the only Savior of the world.

Corbis

Corbis

Divisions in the Church

In a typical community we may find Roman Catholics, Presbyterians, Baptists, Episcopalians, Lutherans, and members of many other church bodies. With opponents of the church showing great strength, it is sad to see Christians divided. As believers joined together in Christ's body through Baptism, we have much in common. As God's Spirit works through the Word, Christians of different denominations love and grow in their understanding and appreciation of one another. As God's people "keep the unity of the Spirit through the bond of peace" (Ephesians 4:3), Christians work together to reach out to unbelievers the world over with the Good News of Jesus, the Son of God and only Savior of the world. Before His crucifixion Jesus prayed "for those who will believe in Me . . . that all of them may be one" (John 17:20–21). In a world that is becoming more pagan every day, Jesus' plea sounds all the more urgent.

The Church's Mission

The main work of the church is to proclaim God's plan of salvation to all people. Jesus said to His disciples: "Go and make disciples of all nations," and: "You will be My witnesses . . . to the ends of the earth."

Approximately two-thirds of the world's present population does not believe in Christ. Today, more than ever before, Christians have the opportunity to testify to all people. Using a variety of global technologies, God has provided means to reach the farthest corners of the earth. He has also given the power of the Gospel to change the hearts of unbelievers. God wants all to be saved (see 1 Timothy 2:4), and every Christian has a part in bringing His will to pass.

1. Have you ever taken part in a religious survey? If so, tell about your experience. Was it like or unlike that of Mary and Shantae?

2. How do you think the people in your neighborhood feel about the Christian church? How might the kind of person you are affect their opinion of the church?

3. "Many Americans—Christians too—seem concerned only with money, sex, and sports." Do you agree with this statement by a Lutheran pastor from Hong Kong? What other things do Christians sometimes put first in their lives? What do you think is the remedy for this situation?

4. What can you personally do to meet the challenge of being different from the world and centering your life in God?

5. How does Christianity differ from all other religions?

6. What can Christians do to help people realize that not all religions are the same?

7. The Christian church today is divided into many denominations. How does this hurt the church's witness and mission work?

8. What advantages do we have in doing mission work that previous generations did not have?

9. With your teacher's help, make a map of the world showing the areas where your church is doing mission work.

10. If possible, talk to a missionary on furlough and find out about his or her work. Report to the class on your interview.

11. If your congregation were given $1 million, how would you recommend that this money be used? List specific projects.

12. Find an article in your daily newspaper or church magazine dealing with some problem confronting the church today. Write a summary of the article and your own comment about the problem.

Prayer

O Holy Spirit, thank You for making me a member of Your church by giving me faith in Jesus. Help me to remain loyal to my Savior and to share His love with others. Amen.

God's Grace through the Ages

Jesus once said to His disciples: "The kingdom of heaven is like a mustard seed, which a man took and planted in his field. Though it is the smallest of all your seeds, yet when it grows, it is the largest of garden plants and becomes a tree, so that the birds of the air come and perch in its branches" (Matthew 13:31–32).

The growth of a mustard seed into a large tree is a good picture of the small beginning and gradual growth of the Christian church. Before He ascended to heaven, our Lord inspired His small group of followers to preach the Gospel in all the world. God blessed the efforts of the first Christians. On Pentecost three thousand men and women received Jesus as their Savior. From Jerusalem the church spread throughout the Roman Empire. Paul was God's great missionary to the Gentiles during this period.

The Early Christians

The early Christians were very much in earnest about their faith. They met frequently for worship and fellowship. Sunday was a special day of worship to commemorate the resurrection of Christ. Bishops were in charge of the congregations, assisted by elders and deacons. One outstanding feature of the Christians was the love they showed one another.

As the church grew, the Roman people and government became disturbed about this "new" religion. Christians rejected the Roman gods and refused to take part in the worship of the emperor. The Romans looked with suspicion at the worship practices and sacraments of the Christians. Gradually persecution developed. Emperors tried to wipe out Christianity. Many followers of the Savior died rather than deny Him. Despite the persecutions, the church continued to grow.

St. Paul by Etienne Parrocel

Lions attacking early Christians in the Roman Colosseum

72

Persecution was stopped when Constantine became emperor. Constantine credited Christ for his key victory over his rivals. As a result he favored the Christian church and gave it special privileges. It was now easy to be a Christian, and some of the early zeal and earnestness disappeared. Constantine often used the church not to fulfill God's purpose, however, but to help maintain his large empire and make himself more powerful.

About a hundred years after Constantine the Roman Empire collapsed. Uncivilized peoples took over the territory, but the church remained strong. It met these changing conditions with a mission spirit. Christians witnessed for Christ among their pagan neighbors. St. Patrick took the Gospel to Ireland. Other missionaries went to Britain and Germany to preach Christ.

As the Roman Empire was collapsing, an important change came about in the organization and leadership of the church. In the early church all bishops were equal. Gradually the bishops in the larger cities came to have a higher rank than those in smaller cities. Finally the bishop of Rome assumed rule over the church and became known as the pope, or father, of the entire church.

Statue of the Virgin Mary with the Infant Jesus, Strasbourg Cathedral, France

The Middle Ages

In the period of history known as the Middle Ages, life centered in God and the church. People looked to the church not only to guide them to heaven but to govern their entire life. The church functioned much as our government does today. It established schools, took care of the needy, and tried to bring about peace between warring groups. Monks made important contributions, especially in the preservation of books. The church also undertook the Crusades to win back the Holy Land from the enemies of Christianity.

Large cathedrals were built in Europe during the Middle Ages. They stand as a monument to a time when the common people looked at life from a Christian point of view. These enormous cathedrals reminded the people that salvation depends on God.

Toward the end of the Middle Ages the spiritual life of many people needed reform. Worldliness had crept into the church. Leaders were more concerned with politics than with serving the church. They shamed the name of Christ with their sinful lives. The common people often used religion as magic. Men like John Wycliffe and Jan Hus protested against these conditions. Hus suffered death because of his stand.

The Reformation

Not until Martin Luther did a real reform start in the church. Luther, worried about his relationship with God, found that the good works demanded by the church gave him little comfort. He even became a monk. Only when he studied the Bible did Luther understand the meaning of Christ's death and resurrection. Later his Ninety-five Theses against the practice of indulgences caused a storm throughout Europe. Luther was excommunicated and condemned, but he stood firm for the Gospel.

Others followed Luther in bringing God's truth back into the church. John Calvin established a Reformation stronghold in Geneva, Switzerland. His *Institutes of the Christian Religion* influenced many Protestants. Denominations that followed Calvin's teachings are

An engraving of Martin Luther defending his writing before Emperor Charles V at the Diet of Worms in 1521

generally referred to as Reformed churches.

After the Reformation, Christians in western Europe no longer belonged to one united church but formed separate church groups. The group led by the pope at Rome became known as the Roman Catholic Church. Many Catholics realized the need for reform in their church. Most influential in this reform was Ignatius Loyola, a Spaniard who dedicated his life to God and the pope. He organized the Society of Jesus, which won back many Protestants to the Catholic faith. The Council of Trent also carried out some reforms in the Roman Church.

Lutherans in Germany were leaders in the Reformation movement. Yet about one hundred years later, reli-gion for many Lutherans had become a formal routine. A number of serious Christians were concerned about living a pious Christian life and were called Pietists. One of their leaders was August Francke. A similar group in England was the Methodists, founded by John and Charles Wesley. Both Pietists and Methodists promoted Bible reading, mission work, and charities.

Lutherans in America

It was through the influence of the Pietists in Germany that Henry Muhlenberg came to America. The greatest Lutheran leader of colonial times, Muhlenberg organized scattered Lutherans in Pennsylvania and neighboring colonies.

Lutherans continued to enter America from Europe throughout the nineteenth century. Many came over to enjoy religious freedom and the separation of church and state. One large group settled in and around St. Louis, Missouri, and another in central Michigan. Under the leadership of C. F. W. Walther the Missouri Synod was organized. The Lutheran Church—

Getty Images

Missouri Synod holds to the entire Bible as the inerrant and inspired Word of God. It teaches the central message of Scripture—salvation by grace through faith in Jesus as the Son of God and Savior of the world. It emphasizes God at work in the lives of people through Word and Sacrament, calling them to faith and empowering and equipping them for lives of Christian service and outreach.

Today the Christian church faces many problems and challenges. Worldliness, indifference, lack of love among Christians, and a lack of missionary zeal are some of the more serious problems. But we know that God's church will triumph and endure, for He said: "The gates of Hades [hell] will not overcome it" (Matthew 16:28).

A. Review Questions

1. How does the parable of the mustard seed illustrate the beginning and growth of the church?

2. What was the importance of Pentecost in the history of the church?

3. How did God change the life of Saul so that he became a great Christian missionary? To which places in the world did Saul (later Paul) travel to preach the Gospel?

4. Why did the Romans persecute the early Christians?

5. Explain: "The blood of the martyrs is the seed of the church."

6. Tell about some of the main features of the early Christians' worship services; their use of the sacraments; and how they lived their faith.

7. What were some of the benefits of Constantine's policy toward the Christian church? What were some of the bad effects?

8. Tell the story of St. Patrick. How does he exemplify the spirit of the church in the days when the Roman Empire was falling apart?

9. Why was the battle of Tours so crucial for Christianity?

10. How does the medieval cathedral illustrate the religious beliefs of people in the Middle Ages?

11. What were some of the contributions of the monks?

12. What were some of the evils in the church during the time of Jan Hus and John Wycliffe?

13. Why is Martin Luther important in the history of the church?

14. Who was another famous leader of the Reformation movement? Which city was the center of his activity?

15. What did the Roman Catholics do to reform their church? What was the main contribution of Ignatius Loyola?

16. What were some of the main achievements of the Pietists and Methodists?

17. What did Henry Muhlenberg do to help the growth of the church in America?

18. Why did the founders of the Missouri Synod come to America?

19. Who was Carl Walther, and what part did he play in the history of the Missouri Synod?

20. What are some of the problems facing the church in our day?

B. Identifying Important Persons

Tell the most important thing you remember about each of these persons.

Peter: _____

_____

Stephen: _____

_____

Polycarp: _____

_____

Arius: _____

_____

Athanasius: _____

_____

Boniface: _____

_____

Bishop Leo: _____

_____

Pope Urban: _____

_____

John Wycliffe: _____

_____

Jan Hus: _____

_____

John Tetzel: _____

_____

William Farel: _____

_____

John Wesley: _____

_____

August Francke: _____

_____

Frederick Wyneken: _____

_____

Wilhelm Löhe: _____

_____

C. Identifying Important Terms and Events

martyr: _____

_____

epistle: _____

_____

bishop: _____

_____

deacon: _____

_____

"In hoc signo vinces": _____

_____

persecution: _____

_____

monastery: _____

_____

Crusades: _____

_____

heretic: _____

_____

Ninety-five Theses: _____

_____

indulgences: _____

_____

Reformation: _____

_____

Society of Jesus: _____

_____

Council of Trent: _____

_____

Methodists: _____

_____

Missouri Synod: _____

_____

D. Identifying Important Places

Jerusalem: _____

_____

Antioch: _____

_____

Rome: _____

_____

Constantinople: _____

_____

Holy Land: _____

_____

Wittenberg: _____

_____

Geneva: _____

_____

Halle: _____

_____

Pennsylvania: _____

_____

Perry County: _____

_____

Time Line

33 A.D. Pentecost

67 Death of Paul

155 Martyrdom of Polycarp

300 Diocletian, last great persecutor

312 Constantine, first Christian emperor

325 Council of Nicaea (Nicene Creed)

432 St. Patrick's mission to Ireland

IRELAND

563 Columba's mission to Scotland

600 Gregory I, bishop of Rome

719 Boniface's mission to Germany

732 Muslims defeated at Tours, France

E. Identifying Important Dates

A.D. 33: _____

_____

325: _____

_____

732: _____

_____

1384: _____

_____

1517: _____

_____

1847: _____

_____

Reformation and Counter-Reformation

800
Charlemagne crowned by pope

1000
Great Cathedrals Built

1096
First Crusade

1384
John Wycliffe's English Bible translation

1415
Death of Jan Hus

1483
Martin Luther born

1517
Luther nails Ninety-five Theses to church door

1536
John Calvin, pastor in Geneva

1540
Ignatius Loyola organizes Society of Jesus

1687
Beginning of Pietist Movement

1742
Henry Muhlenberg comes to Pennsylvania

1847
Missouri Synod organized

Today
Christianity is the world's largest religion with more than two billion followers of Christ.

1545–63
Council of Trent

1729
Beginning of Methodist Movement

1839
Martin Stephan and Saxons come to St. Louis

1980–present
New media, television and the Internet, help bring the love of Christ to the world.